HARNESSING THE
SUN'S ENERGY

HARNESSING THE SUN'S ENERGY

COMBINATION OF ART AND RENEWABLE ENERGY

ENGR. JULIAN KELECHI IGBO

SOLAR RENEWABLE/ALTERNATIVE ENERGY

To my mother, the late Madam Justina M. Igbo, whose memory remains always evergreen, and those who fight for peace, unity, progress, and education for all

CONTENTS

The improvements in standards of living and the protection of our environment have led mankind to harness the sun's energy and utilize energy sources that do not pollute the environment. One cannot always rely on fossil energy.

Fossil energy comes from animals and plants that died millions of years ago. However, fossil fuels are not friendly to human beings and the environment. Thus solar, alternative/renewable energy, is termed the energy of the future.

The author's inspirations are directed towards helping humankind understand the value of protecting human beings and our environment. Harnessing energy from the sun and accepting that we cannot always depend on fossil energy is quite a positive initiative. Many people think that when there is no war or when there is no destructions, there is "peace." However, when we are positively protecting our environment, we are positively making peace.

This book is therefore a simplified version of solar, alternative/renewable energy, which realistically will appeal to students and many other people invaluably.

With my engineering knowledge acquired from European Energy Centre, Edinburgh Napier University, Scotland, and the Energieakademie Toggenburg, Wattwil Switzerland, I positively recommend this book for students and many people who want to benefit from solar alternative/renewable energy, both practically and theoretically.

PREFACE

The impact of solar/renewable energy in creating a fossil-free environment and for the comfort of human beings is something to write home about. Renewable energy, as an alternative in energy usage, has given way to a pollution-free environment and created job opportunities in many fields.

I think renewable energy should find its maximum acceptance in the tropics. The problem one encounters is the exorbitant prices of the available materials. I feel that workshops, seminars, training, and introduction of renewable energy courses in institutions will pave the way to a positive role in development, protection of our environment, and alleviation of some problems in rural areas.

The book is therefore mainly written to help students and professionals have practical and theoretical knowledge about solar/renewable energy. The book is simplified, with a less rigorous approach in writing the text. The System International (SI) Units have also been used throughout the text. However, it is also assumed that the reader has the background of ordinary level physics, chemistry, mathematics, and biology.

J. K. Igbo
Switzerland

ACKNOWLEDGEMENTS

I wish to acknowledge the revered assistance of a number of people for contributing to the successful production of this book.

My sincere thanks are expressed to the Green Organisation for the good work they are doing to protect our environment.

I would also like to express my thanks to the European Energy Centre, Edinburgh, UK; Energieakademie Toggenburg Wattwil, Switzerland; and the Federal University of Technology, Owerri, Nigeria, where I got invaluable experiences both practically and theoretically.

I also wish to acknowledge the efforts my family has been offering me to see that I move forward in a positive direction.

I wholly acknowledge the support of Bina Nold Igbo, Olivia, Rich, Val, and Uchechi Ezinne Chisom, who made sure I never relented in my efforts towards success and who supported me positively and moved me towards thoughtful issues. My deepest regards to them.

I wish to acknowledge the immense support of Jury Donath and his family.

My great thanks are also extended to Professor Ogbobe, Federal University of Technology, Owerri, Nigeria; Engineer Augustine Madumere, Marketing Intelligence & CRM, Zurich, Switzerland; Mark Oguh, financial controller of Diamond Bank Nigeria.

I am also indebted to those who make peace, those who protect the environment, and people who extend hands to make sure quality education is accessible for all.

CHAPTER 1

Brief History of Energy and the Environment

Man has utilized energy for millions of years. During the Stone Ages, stones were used to produce fire for light, heat for cooking, and so many other energy-related tasks.

We have other types of energy, such as fossil energy, which is derived from animals and plants that died millions of years ago. Usage of fossil fuel gives rise to global warming and climatic changes. Protection of our environment is one of the basic things one has to bear in mind.

When we talk of peace, many people may define it as lack of war and the resultant destruction. When the environment is free from pollution, we drink clean water, live in a clean and conducive environment, and have peace.

For this, we should vehemently adhere to the rules and regulations of environmental protections to keep our environment safe.

The application and usage of renewable/alternative energy should be given more attention for the protection of our environment.

CHAPTER 2

Renewable/Alternative Energy

When we talk of renewable energy, we are talking about energy of the future. This future energy is a friendly energy that does not pollute the environment.

Most of these energy works are related to Albert Einstein's law: $\Sigma = mc^2$. E is the energy content. M is the mass of an object or system. C is constant, the speed of light.

We cannot always rely on fossil energy because most dangerous gases such as CO (carbon monoxide) and others emanate from fossil fuels, thereby polluting the environment and contributing to environmental hazards. This makes renewable/alternative energy take a solid stand.

CHAPTER 3

Energy

What is energy? Energy is simply defined as the ability to do work. Work done is force times distance. This is equivalent to NM (newton metre). W = f x d = NM = joules. When the distance is represented by S, work done is equal to f x d, which is f x s = NM.

Consider an object with mass (M) over a platform and of height (H) as represented below:

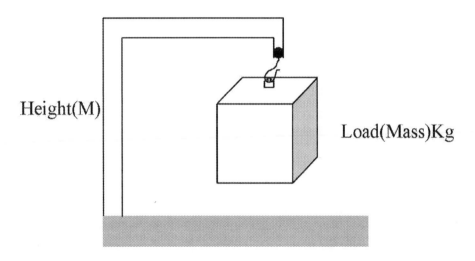

Height(M) = Height in meters

F = ma
M = mass
A = acceleration due to gravity
Here, the work done is equivalent to F x H. *F* = force, and *H* = height (perpendicular). Work done also can be mgh, mass x g x h, which implies mass (kg) x gravitational force x height.

Quantity of Heat can be defined as mass times the coefficient of heat times temperature change.
Q = M.C .Dt

Eg. One kg of water is being boiled from 0 °C to 100 °C is equal to 100kg of (H2O) water being boiled from 0 °C to 1°C

Q = m.c.dt = 1kg x 4.2j / kg k x 100k = 420 KJ

Power

P = Power, which is expressed in watt (W)

Power P = W/t = work done / time

This is equivalent to E/ Time = NM/S = J/S

Where E = Energy

Therefore, J/S is equivalent to watt.

Kinds of Energy

- Kinetic energy

- Mechanical energy

- Sound energy

- Thermal energy

- Chemical energy

- Electrical energy

- Gravitational energy

- Radiant energy

- Warehouses, stores transfer, and dissipation

Stored Energy

One of the ways of storing energy is in the form of chemical energy in batteries. When connected to a circuit, energy stored in the battery will be released to generate electricity.

The battery has a positive and negative terminal. When you connect the terminals with wire, then you have created a circuit and electrons will start flowing through the wire to generate electricity.

We can also store energy in different ways—such as in food, gasoline, wind-up alarm clocks, water, thermo flasks—and this can be transferred into other kinds of energy too.

A typical example is the energy stored in a matchstick (fig. 1) and the simplest possible climatic model (fig. 2) below.

Fig. 1 below

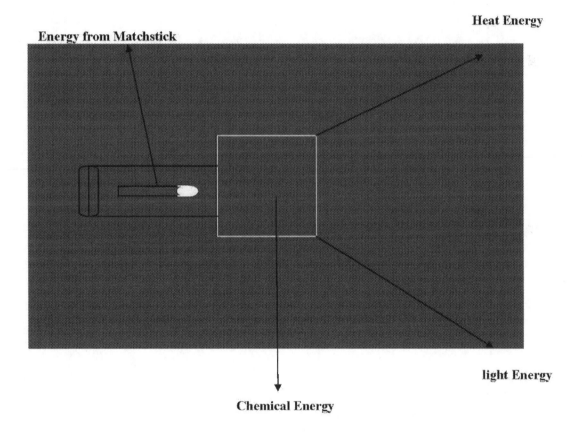

Fig. 2 below

Fig. 2 is a typical example of energy movement.

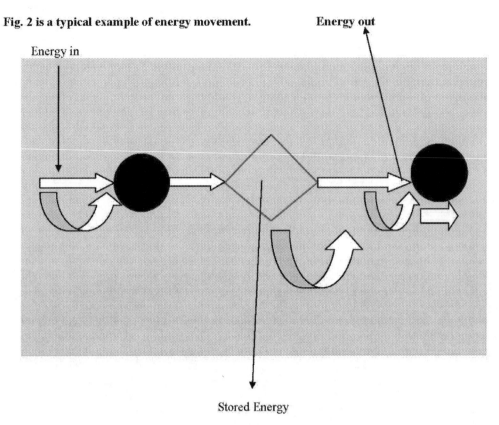

Transferring Kinetic Energy from Snooker Stick to the Ball

When you hit a snooker ball with a snooker cue (stick), you are transferring kinetic energy from the cue to the ball, which has potential energy due to position.

When the ball rolls, one notices that its kinetic energy reduces as it gradually stops.

When you slide a snooker ball on the table, it moves quickly and then slowly comes to a stop. This implies that the kinetic energy of the ball reduces and eventually comes to a zero position when the ball stops or comes to a rest. With zero external force on the pool table, the energy of the ball must be conserved.

What happened to the kinetic energy? The kinetic energy has been dissipated through frictional forces.

Examples of kinetic energy transferring from stick to ball are shown below.

THE SNOOKER

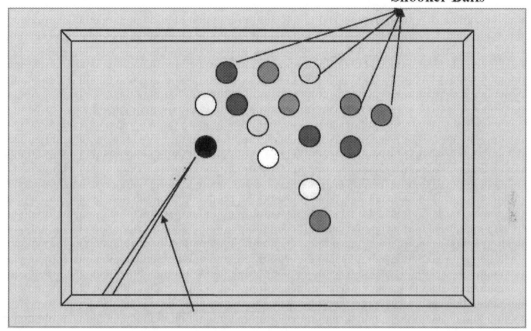

Snooker Balls

Snooker Stick

Energy at Work

When you look at the diagram below, you notice energy at work.

In the Energy system, work is done and heat is also produced.

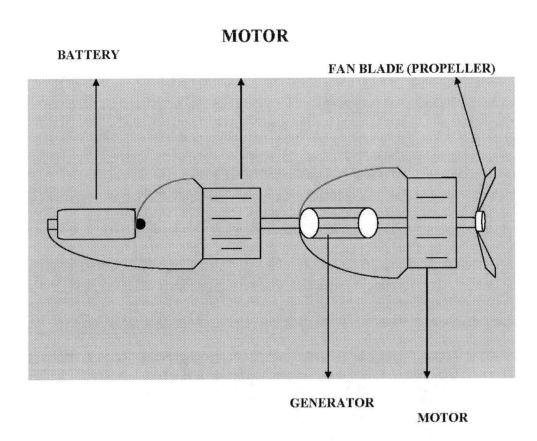

Fig.4

This is a typical example of things working together and making movements, entailing that energy is involved.

Energy helps motors to move, helps propellers to rotate, helps cars to move on the road, helps one ride bicycles, and so forth.

We need energy for our body mechanisms; energy also helps plants to grow.

Furthermore, with the help of energy, we are able to play music on the radio, light our homes, and watch television.

Below are other examples.

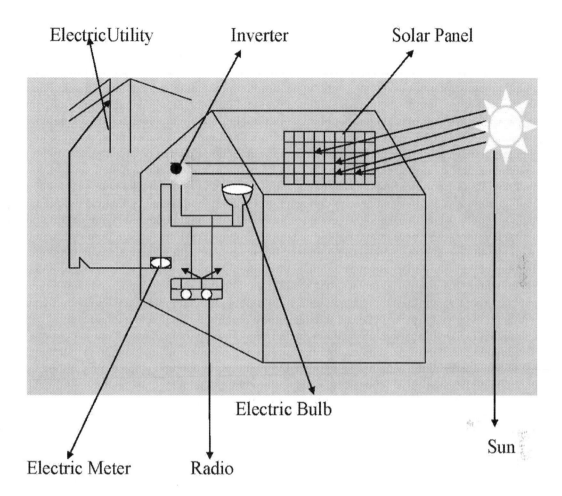

Fig.5

Energy Stored or Transferred

We can transfer or store energy from one place to another or from object to object.

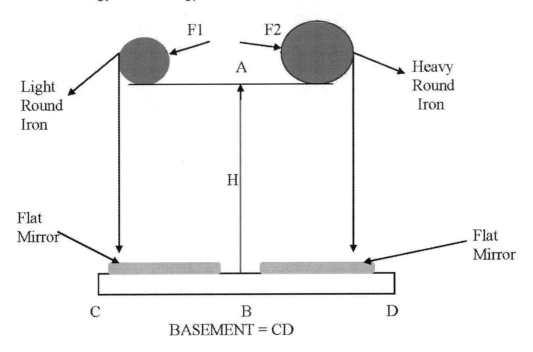

KINETIC ENERGY

Kinetic Energy is the Energy absorbed due to movement or motion

AB = The Height, F1 and F2 are the applied forces on the round (Light) and (Heavy) Iron materials.

Fig.6

Kinetic Energy

Kinetic energy is the energy absorbed due to movement or motion

F1 F2 are the applied forces

Height = H

Flat Mirros M1 and M2

Basement = CD

AB = The height, F1, and F2 are the applied forces on the round (light) and (heavy) iron materials.

When the iron balls are pushed down, you will find out that the heavy iron ball will have the most impact on the flat glass mirror.

- Initially, both iron balls have PE, which is potential energy.

- For having a height apart, they also have gravitational energy acting on them.

- Furthermore, by falling off the table, they must have acquired or changed from PE and gravitational energy to kinetic energy (KE).

- Other examples are rotating fans, moving cars, diving in swimming pools, and so forth.

Mechanical Energy

When work is done, mechanical energy comes in. However, the sum of kinetic and potential energy in an object or objects that are used to do work is the mechanical energy. Therefore, it is the energy in an object due to motion or position.

Sound Energy

The movement of energy through substances in longitudinal waves (rarefaction/compression).
When a force causes an object or substance to vibrate, energy is transferred through the substance in a waveform.
The energy is very small compared to other forms of energy.

The figure below shows how sound wave is represented.

DIAGRAM OF SOUND WAVES

Displacement (m)

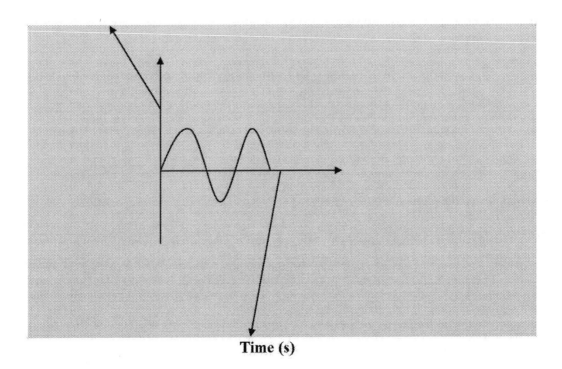

Time (s)

Fig.7

WAVE FORM

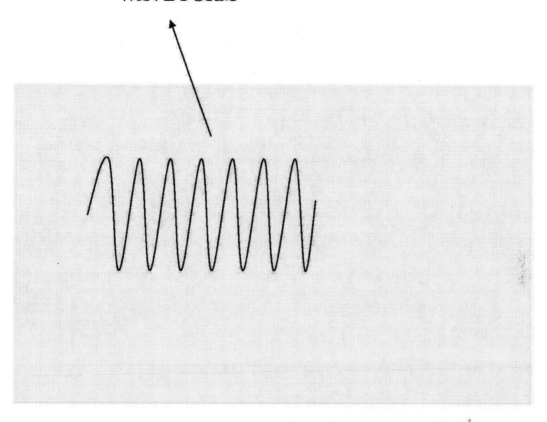

Fig. 8

Wave Form

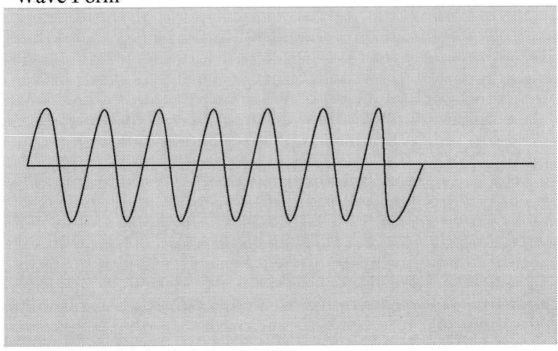

Fig.9

Sound energy is measured by its pressure and intensity in special units known as pascals and decibels.

Note that very loud noise can cause great damage or pain to people—for example, damage to house glass (windows and doors) due to resonance.

Threshold: When sound causes pain to people, we call it threshold of pain, and it depends on individuals.

Fig 10

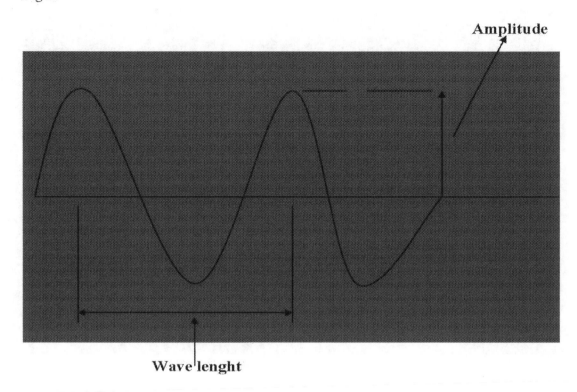

Observing the structures of musical notes and noise, one finds out that they have different structural forms

Noise

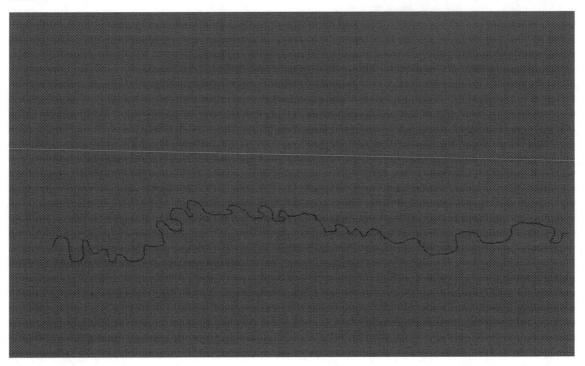

Musical note

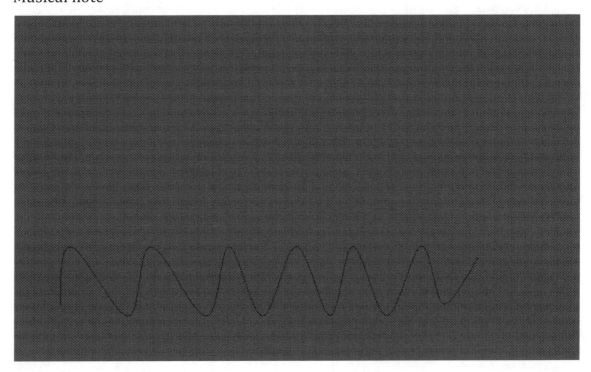

Thermal Energy (Heat)

Matter is anything that has weight and occupies space. Matter is made up of particles or molecules that move or vibrate constantly. When the temperature of matter is energized, the particles vibrate very fast. Therefore, thermal energy is the energy that comes from the temperature of the matter.

The molecules vibrate more when the matter receives more heat. For instance, when you prepare hot tea, it will be hot, but after some time, it becomes cooler and cooler. When you add milk to it, it will lose more heat because it has given out thermal energy to the milk.

The amount of thermal energy is measured in joules (J).

Temperature

Heat and temperature are definitely not the same.

When you measure how hot or cold an object is in degrees Celsius, then we talk of temperature. The temperature can also be measured in Kelvin or Fahrenheit scale.

In Fahrenheit scale, water freezes at 32 °F and boils at 212°F. On the Celsius scale, water boils at 100 °C and freezes at O °C.

Heating of Water in Two Different Bowls (Typical Example)

Heating of water in two different bowls is a typical example of thermal energy.

$$H^+ + H^+ + O^-$$

H_2O ⟶ H^+

                    O^-

        H^+

Solute combined with Solvent ⟶ Solution

grannules of salt in bowl
(Solute)

grannules of salt +water

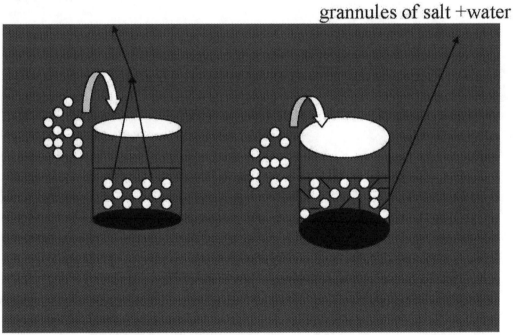

water is the solvent

$$Concentration = \frac{\textbf{Solute}}{\textbf{Solvent}}$$

Fig.11

From the figure above, the concentration of the water solution is as follows: concentration = solute/solvent.

When one starts to heat water, the molecules will start to be in random motion.

When water starts to boil in bowl A and bowl B to a level 100 °C and then you leave or stop heating, you will find out that bowl A will cool more easily than bowl B. This is because B has more thermal energy due to the volume and quantity of water inside it.

A

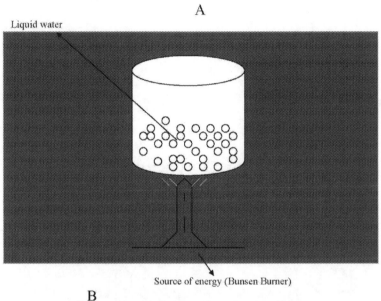

Liquid water

Source of energy (Bunsen Burner)

B

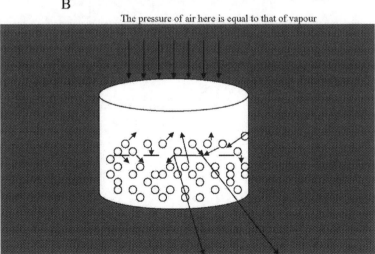

The pressure of air here is equal to that of vapour

The bubbles are In a state of random motion

Fig. 12

CHAPTER 4

Conduction, Convection, and Radiation

We can transfer heat from one place to the other, from particles to the other, or from one object to the other object. This is done through conduction, convection, and radiation.

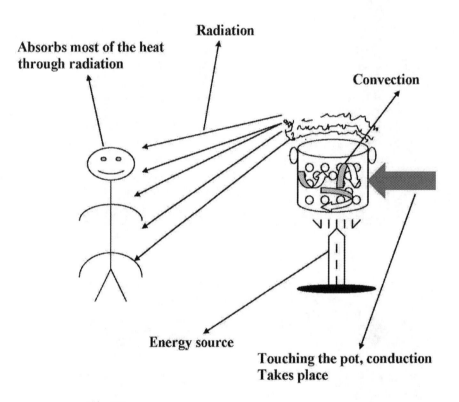

Fig.13

The cat absorbs most of its heat from the sun through radiant energy.

Proportion of heat loss and the speed of Wind

Y-Axis (heat loss)

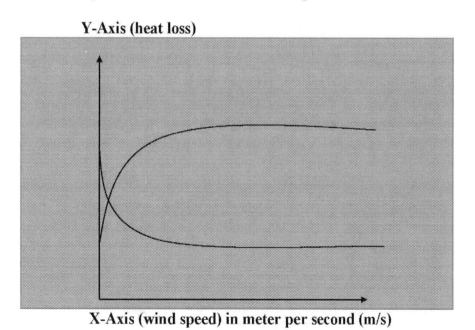

X-Axis (wind speed) in meter per second (m/s)

Fig.14

Proportion of Heat Loss and Wind Speed, M/S.

The sun and radiation energy

Sun

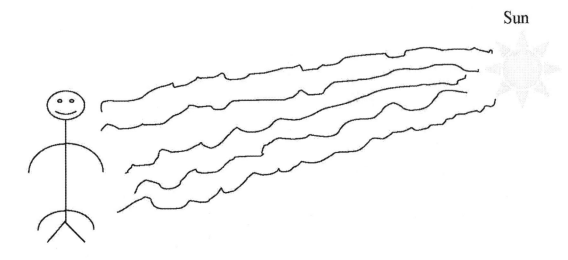

Fig.15

CHAPTER 5

Chemical Energy

When energy is stored in bonds of chemical compounds (atoms and molecules) during chemical reactions, this energy is released, producing heat (exothermic reaction). Biomass, batteries, petroleum, natural gas, and coal are typical examples of stored chemical energy.

For instance, when an explosive is let loose, chemical energy stored is transferred to the surroundings as thermal energy, sound energy, and kinetic energy.

Another example is using wood pellets. A dry wood pellet is a good example of stored chemical energy. When it burns, chemical energy is released and converted to thermal heat and light energy, which turns the wood into a different substance.

A sketch of wood pellets burning

Fig.16

pellet-plants.com

Types of wood pellets

Corn stalk

Branches from wood

Husk from rice

Saw dust

Cut chips from wood

Cut sections from wheat

Wood or biomass pellet materials serve as renewable, clean-burning, and cost-effective home heating alternative energy.

Electrical Energy

Atoms contribute to matter. In these atoms are tiny electrons that are in constant motion. These movements depend on the amount of energy it has. This signifies that every object has potential energy.

Conductors carry energy along. When a material cannot carry energy along, it is called an insulator. Furthermore, we generate electrical energy when electrons move from one point to the other with the means of magnetic forces. An electron is a negatively charged subatomic particle. It can be free, not attached to the atom or bound to the centre or nucleus of an atom. Electrons are spherical shells of radii representing different energy levels.

Electrical energy can be used for work or stored.

Example.1

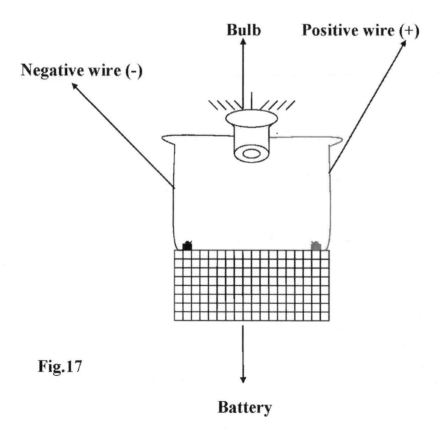

Fig.17

Example 2

The Electron, Proton, Neutron and the Nucleus Orbit

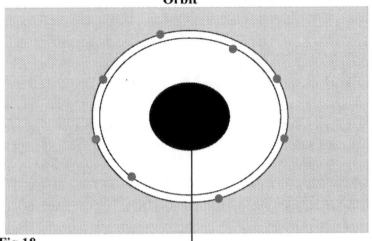

Fig.18

Nucleus

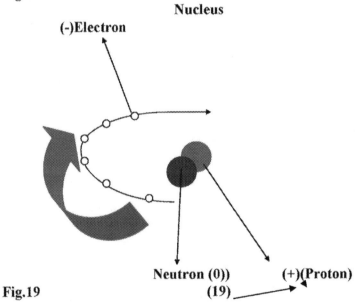

(-)Electron

Fig.19

Neutron (0))
(19)

(+)(Proton)

Neutron (0) no net electric charge.
Proton 19 for instance potassium (K) in the periodic table
Atomic number is **19**
Number of protons **19**

{ **2, 8, 8, 1** }

Energy Levels

First energy level	**2**
Second energy level	**8**
Third energy level	**8**
Fourth energy level	**1**

CHAPTER 6

Gravitational Energy

Gravitational energy is energy due to the height of an object. When an object is placed high up, a force is likely to be holding it at the state of its position.

When you are lifting an object at a constant velocity, the force you are applying to lift is equal to the weight of the object (gravitational force).

V = constant

Round moulded concrete object pulled up

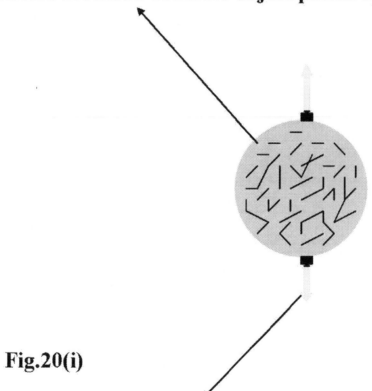

Fig.20(i)

Gravitational force acts downwards

Therefore, the net force here is equal to zero

The height is the distance from horizontal of the height base to the exact point where the arrow touches the shoe (Rain boot).

Shoe (Rain boot)

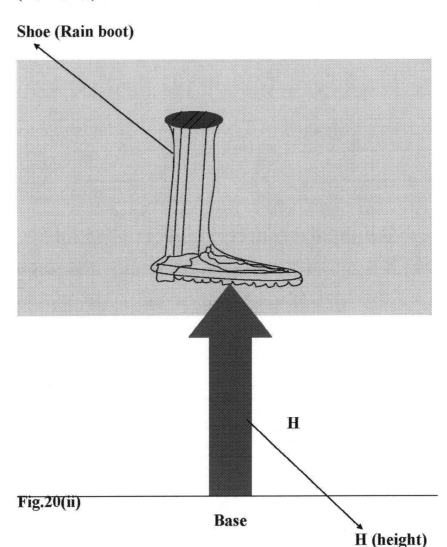

H

Fig.20(ii)

Base

H (height)

The height is the distance from the horizontal of the height base to the point the arrow touches the shoe.

The distance over which the force acts is the height through which the object is lifted.

Gravitational Potential Energy

The energy that is stored in the gravitational field is known as gravitational potential energy or potential energy due to gravity. One has to remember that the work done is force times distance.

W = F. d

Sketch of force pulling a moulded block with a force equal to weight of the material

Moulded block

SKETCH OF FORCE PULLING A MOULDED BLOCK WITH A FORCE EQUAL TO WEIGHT OF THE MATERIAL

Eg. 1a,

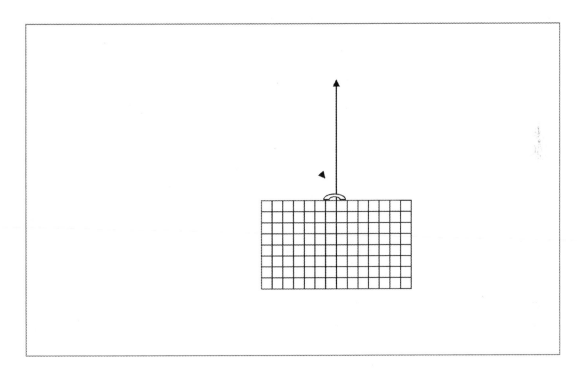

MOULDED BLOCK

Fig.21(i)

Force (pulling of block up)

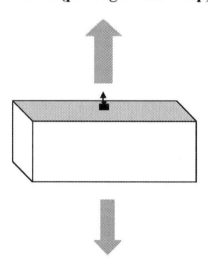

There is also force of gravity acting downwards

Here, the force applied in lifting the object is equal to the weight of the object. This implies that F= ma = mass x g. Then work done is the force applied times the displacement (height or distance).

W = F. d
W = mgh

The work is now stored energy. This work which is done on the object when it is lifted does not end as energy of motion or kinetic energy, because after the lift, the object is not moving again. It becomes stationary and is placed up. Then we say that the energy has been stored in the gravitational field. This stored energy is known as potential energy. Since it is energy in a gravitational field, it is called gravitational potential energy or potential energy due to gravity = Ug = mgh in joules.

Calculate the gravitational potential energy for a 10 kg object that is lifted or raised 7.5 m

Ug = mgh, which is 10 kg x 9.8 m/s/s x 7.5m = 735J

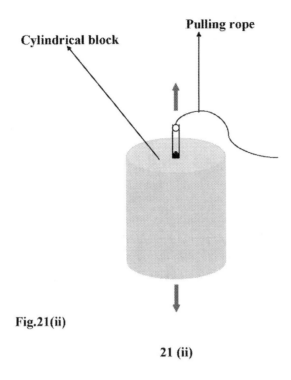

Cylindrical block

Pulling rope

Fig.21(ii)

21 (ii)

Elastic Potential Energy

This is the energy stored in elastic materials because of their stretching or compressing. Elastic potential energy can be stored in rubber bands, trampolines, springs, and so forth. The more stretch, the more stored energy.

The other example is an arrow drawn in a bow. It also has stored potential energy.

The other example is the structure of the bow drawn below pulling the string and the arrow in a bow.

Here, there is force due to pulling and also stored potential energy.

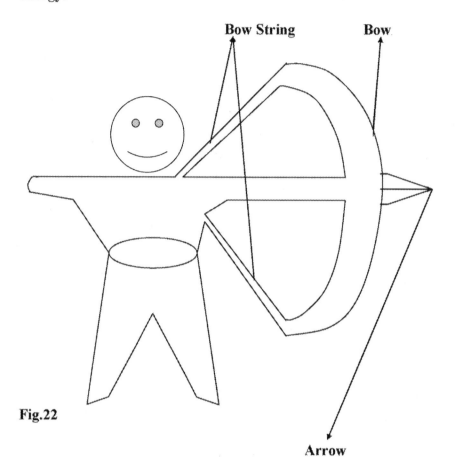

Bow String   **Bow**

Fig.22

Arrow

Kinetic Energy Formula

When an object has motion, vertical or horizontal, it has kinetic energy. We have different kinds of kinetic energy.

- Vibrational energy

- Translational energy

- Rotational energy

KE = ½ m v^2 is the kinetic energy formula.

Where m is the mass, v is the speed of the object. Velocity or speed from the equation can also be calculated.

$K = \frac{1}{2} m v^2$

From the above formula:

$2k = mv^2$

$m = 2k/v^2$

v^2 equals $2k/m$

Then v = square root of $2k/m$

$V = \sqrt{2k/m}$

CHAPTER 7

Solar Energy/Solar Photovoltaics

Renewable energy comes from natural resources like sunlight, wind, rain, and geothermal heat. This is the energy of the future and does not pollute the environment.

When we speak of renewable energy, we are talking about its technology, ranging from solar power, biomass, biofuels for transportation, wind power, and hydroelectricity/micro hydro.

Alternative energy is an energy source that is used in place of fossil fuels and has low environmental impacts. Alternative energy does not harm the environment.

Biomass is renewable organic matter such as biological materials derived from living organisms. Materials like wood, wastes, and alcohol fuels are examples. We also have biomass alcohol derived from corn.

Wood energy is from wood and waste wood products harvested as fuel.

One can also derive waste energy from municipal waste products, landfill gas, and wastes from manufacturing companies.

Biodiesel is derived from plant oils and can be used in diesel engines. It is made from renewable organic raw materials like rapeseed oils, waste vegetable oils, soya beans, animal fats, and microalgae oils.

Furthermore, most renewable energy comes directly from the sun or solar energy.

Solar Energy

Most renewable energy sources come directly or indirectly from the sun or solar energy. They can be used for heating, lighting of homes, generating electricity, boiling of water, solar cooling, and so many other things.

Some other renewable energy sources do not directly come from the sun. Geothermal energy collects the earth's internal heat for many uses, such as electric power production and heating and cooling of buildings.

The energy of ocean tides is from the gravitational pull of the moon and the sun on the earth. Furthermore, ocean energy can also be from the ocean waves, which are driven by ocean tides and winds.

Mostly the sun strikes and warms the surface of the ocean more than the depth of the ocean, which can be used to determine the temperature difference—surface and depth temperature difference.

CHAPTER 8

Photovoltaics (PV)

(PV) Photovoltaics generate electric power by means of converting the sun's rays into direct current using semiconducting materials that exhibit the photovoltaic effect.

When combined together, a number of cells produce solar panels or modules which supply solar power. A single solar cell produces only about half a volt. Therefore, twelve will produce about twenty-four solar cells.

A solar panel does not make use of the heat from the sun but rather from the energy of the sun's rays. The power supplied by solar panels is clean energy (sustainable energy).

Heat destroys solar panels. When a solar panel has a crack or is broken due to an object that falls on it, there are frictional forces and heat is generated at this particular point, known as a hot spot.

Solar cells produce direct current electricity from the rays of the sun, which can be used to charge a battery, and the energy is stored in the battery too.

Solar modules are available in different power ratings or outputs, cell technology, frame types, and the life expectance and its efficiency. These factors determine the best panel to suit one's needs.

Solar panels can be produced in different colours to create distinctive looks for either security or architectural reasons. The production of modules in different colours is also due to custom trademark reasons. During production of solar panels, the colour to be added must be calculated because more or excess addition of colours to the solar cells will result in the degradation of the performance of the normal cells by about 20 per cent.

PV and Cold

Does PV work in cold? The answer is yes. PVs generate power at low temperatures, other factors being equal. PVs generate electricity from light rays, not heat, and operate more efficiently at cooler temperatures.

PVs will generate less energy in winter than in summer; this is due to shorter days, lower sun angles, and more cloud cover.

CHAPTER 9

PV Module Efficiency Rating

Solar modules are rated at a well-defined set of conditions known as standard test conditions (STC). These conditions include the temperature of the PV cells (25 C or 77 F), the intensity of radiation (1 kw/square metre), and the spectral distribution of the light at air mass 1.5, or AM 1.5, which is the spectrum of the sunlight that has been filtered by passing through 1.5 thickness of the earth's atmosphere.

During production, PV modules are tested in chambers known as flash simulators.

The device has a flashbulb and filter designed to mimic sunlight as closely as possible. Its accuracy is about 1.3 per cent.

The flash takes place in about fifty milliseconds and does not heat up the cells. The ambient temperature of the module/factory is usually close to 25 °C, the standard temperature.

There is an energy efficiency range for different kinds of panels.

Cell Type Efficiency Range

Monocrystalline silicon cells 14 to 16 per cent

Polycrystalline silicon cells 13 to 15 per cent

However, some higher efficiency monocrystalline cells are about 16.5 per cent.

CHAPTER 10

PV Module Life Circle

The PV modules are the longest-living component of the PV system. High-quality modules are designed to last at least thirty years but carry a warranty of twenty to twenty-five years. They are designed to withstand all the rigours of the environment.

These rigours include Arctic cold, snow, desert, tropical humidity, wind in excess of 125 miles per hour (55.88m/s) and one-inch (25 mm) hail at terminal velocity.

High-quality industrial batteries are produced to last about seven years, while smaller sealed units will last for about three to five years. Automotive batteries are not good for PV systems.

Watt Peak (WP)

The watt peak represents the maximum amount of energy the solar panel can pump out on an ideal day, which is early afternoon on a sunny day. Furthermore, the actual wattage the solar panels produce varies day by day, depending on how much sunshine reaches or strikes the panels.

Cloudiness or fogginess can deter solar panel efficiency. Seasons are also factors.

The time of the day is a factor too. Furthermore, the angle of the panels affects how much sun they get and how much power they will produce.

The watt peak is just a reference point you can use to compare other types of solar panels. Industrial standards are used to calculate this.

Typical Solar Cells

Typical solar cells are arranged in a module to produce voltages in increments of twelve, twenty-four, and thirty-six volts. The trend is towards high-voltage modules.

Some factors to be considered before mounting solar panels:

- Consider the area

- Check if the solar panels respond to ultraviolet blue light

- See how solid the solar panels are

- Consider the solar angle

- Consider reflection lapses

- Make sure that the surface of the solar panels are clean

- Make sure there is no application of heat

- Make provisions for air entrance

- Give attention to solid bases while installing

- Consider stress/strain tests before mounting

- Ensure good aluminium housing of the solar panels

- Make sure your solar array system is well earthed

- Consider good anti-reflective glass (tempered glass) coating

- Make sure your solar panels are not shaded to avoid reduction in output of the power

Grid and off-Grid System

Let us discuss grid and off-grid connected power generation. Grid is a technique whereby the power that is coming from an off-grid set-up can also be used and the excess can supply power to a national power system or external power supply system. An example is the National Electric Power Authority (NEPA), whereby at a stage you may not pay an electric bill due to excess power from your off-grid system supplied to them.

Remember, during installation of solar modules, when you are not facing the right direction, you lose a lot of power.

Off-Grid System

Fig.23(i)

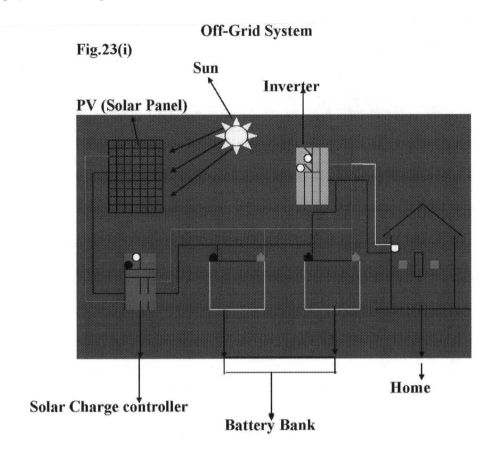

Fig. A Off-Grid System

Fig.23(ii)

Grid-System

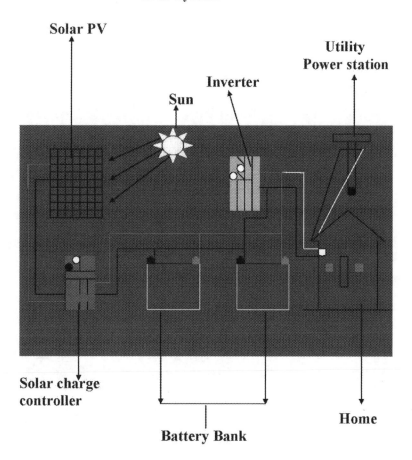

Fig. B Grid System

Solar Angle Direction Sketches

Fig.24

Solar Angle Direction Sketches

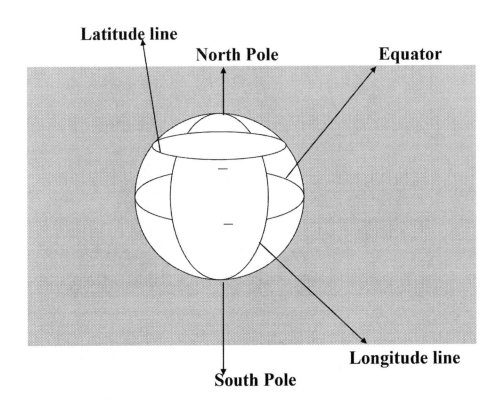

Latitude line • North Pole • Equator • Longitude line • South Pole

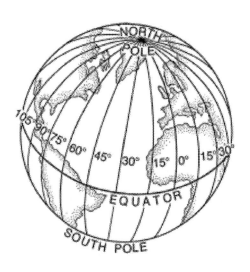

en.wikipedia.org

THE DIAGRAMS ABOVE SHOW THE LINES OF
LONGITUDE, LATITUDE AND THE EQUATOR.

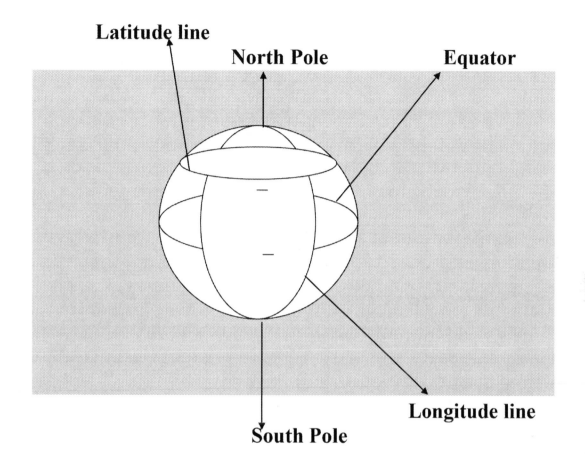

Latitude line

North Pole

Equator

Longitude line

South Pole

Fig.25

Solar Angle Direction SE

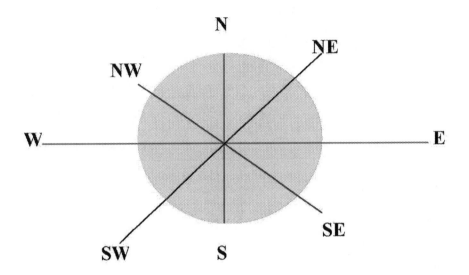

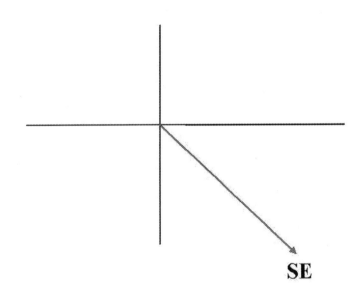

Fig.26

Solar Angle Direction SE

CHAPTER 11

Maximum Power Point (MPPT)/Peak Power (VPP)

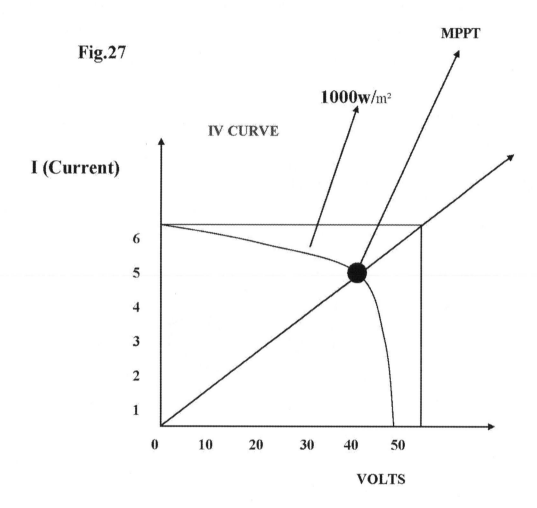

Fig.27

MPPT

1000w/m²

IV CURVE

I (Current)

VOLTS

MPPT Controller

The PV module's ideal voltage is that which can produce a maximum power output. This point is called maximum power point or peak power voltage. VPP varies with sunlight intensity and with solar cell temperature. In other to charge the battery, increase its voltage.

Furthermore, the PV module must apply a voltage that is higher than that of the battery.

When the PV module's VPP (or MPPT) is just slightly below the battery voltage, then the current drops to nearly zero.

For safety purposes, typical PV modules are made to be around seventeen volts when measured at a cell temperature of 25 °C. This is so because it will drop around fifteen volts on a very hot day. Furthermore, on a very cold day, it can rise to eighteen volts.

The MPPT varies the ratio between current and the voltage delivered to the battery in order to deliver maximum power.

Note that if there is excess voltage in PV, then it converts that additional current to the battery.

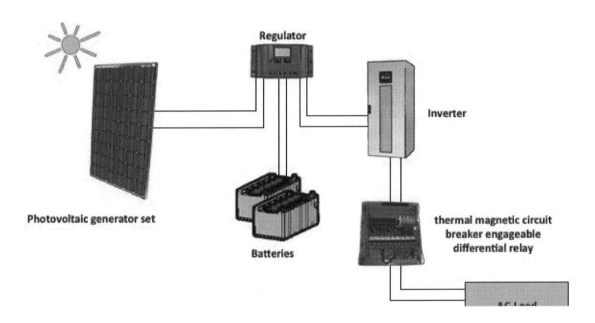

www.cenitsolar.com

Air Mass

At Equator the Am=1
In Europa the Am=1.5

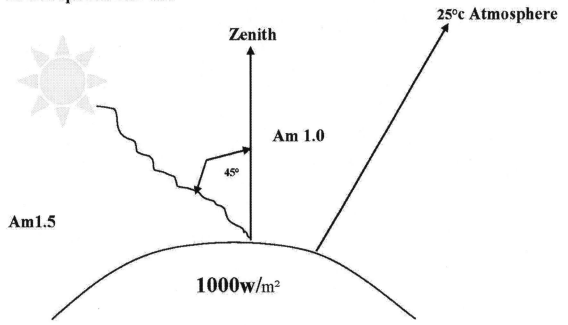

Fig.28

CHAPTER 12

Active and Passive Solar Energy Systems

One can get solar energy directly from the sun through passive solar energy and active solar energy systems.

The ancient people used passive solar energy systems to build their houses out of stones and clay. The stones or clay materials absorbed the sun's heat during the day, and the houses stayed warm during the night, providing heat throughout the evening.

Building architects use this system to build passive houses to capture solar energy.

For instance, they construct houses with double- and triple-paned doors or windows that get direct sunlight and retain the sun's warmth.

Furthermore, when a car is parked outside on a sunny day, it absorbs sun energy from the windows and traps it. Thus the air inside becomes much warmer than the air outside.

Active Solar Energy System

An active solar energy system is another means of energy capture, using the same system of passive solar energy except that the active solar energy system uses fluid such as water to absorb the heat. A solar collector positioned on the top roof of a building heats the fluid and pumps it through a system of pipes to heat up the building.

Active Solar Energy System Sketch

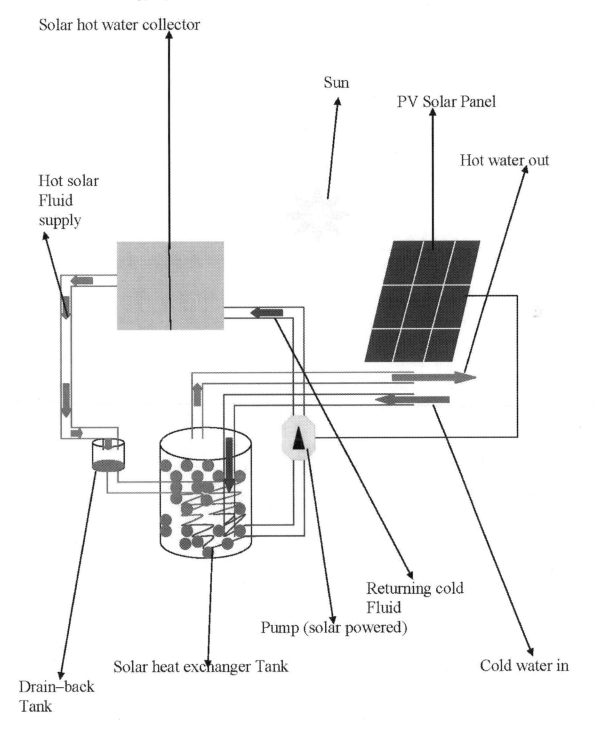

Solar hot water collector

Sun

PV Solar Panel

Hot water out

Hot solar
Fluid
supply

Returning cold
Fluid

Pump (solar powered)

Cold water in

Solar heat exchanger Tank

Drain–back
Tank

Fig.29

Passive Solar Energy

Passive energy is more sustainable than the active energy systems because passive systems use fewer natural resources to build and maintain.

They do not rely so heavily on gas for heating or coolants for air conditioning. A passive solar energy building should be designed to receive as much southern sun as possible.

In summer, the hot sun can be shaded by using overhangs or trees.

Passive Solar Energy Sketch

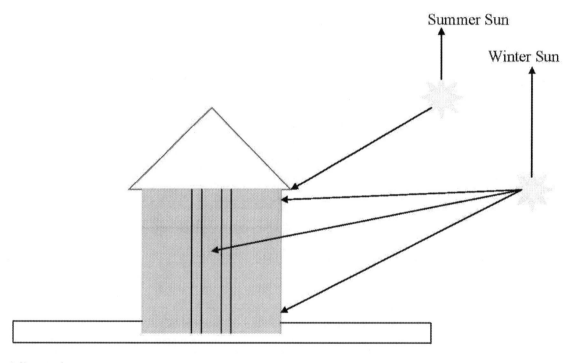

Fig.30

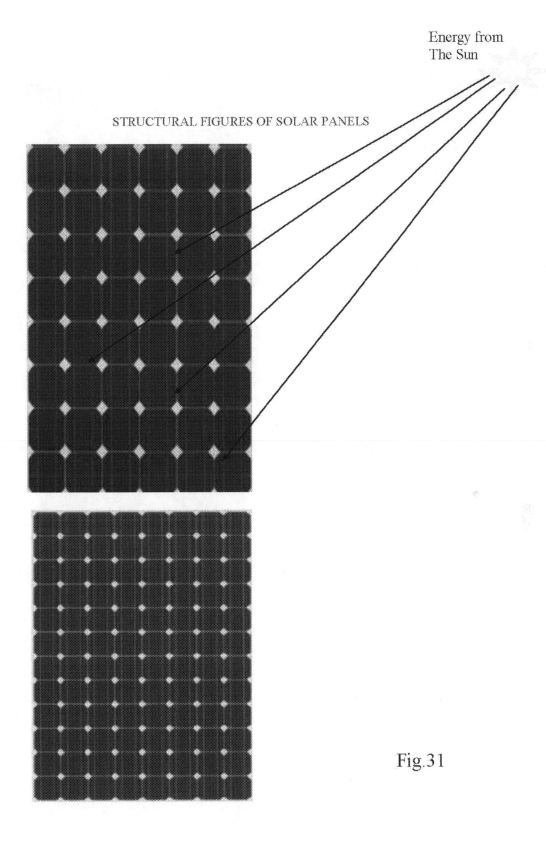

STRUCTURAL FIGURES OF SOLAR PANELS

Energy from
The Sun

Fig.31

Bluesun Solar

SOLAR PANEL ARRAY

Fig.32

CHAPTER 13

Structural Figures of Solar Panels

Mono Crystalline and Poly Crystalline Solar Modules

Fig.33

Mono Crystalline Solar Panel

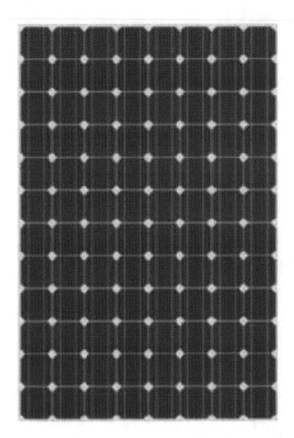

Fig.34

Poly Crystalline Solar Panel

Look at the solar panels above and identify the differences and make small notes.

Polycrystalline and Monocrystalline Solar Modules

Polycrystalline and Monocrystalline Solar Modules

Polycrystalline Module

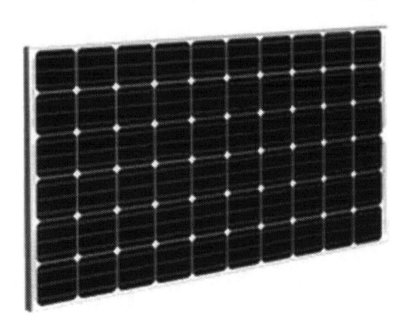

Monocrystalline Module

Please look at the solar panels above and identify the differences, making notes about them.

Solar Energy Project Work Carried out in Nigeria

The first solar tree in Africa is a combination of art and renewable energy. It was installed in Nigeria in Area 11, opposite the Nigeria Television Authority.

The solar tree has flowers and leaves for decoration and good aesthetics.

The solar tree has thirty-six branches and symbolises one love, peace, and unity of Nigeria.

This first solar tree in Africa is made of renewable energy LED floodlights and customized solar modules and is automatically operated.

The solar tree detects when it is night and starts immediately around six thirty in the evening, and when the weather is clear in the morning, around six thirty, it goes off.

Furthermore, you can check out the first solar tree in Africa on Facebook or Google it.

**THE FIRST SOLAR TREE IN AFRICA, A COMBINATION OF ART AND RENEWABLE
ENERGY**

Project Engr. Julian Igbo (MEEC) Member European Energy Centre.
Fig.35

The first solar tree in Africa (a combination of art and renewable energy)

CHAPTER 14

Angle/Tilt Positions

To calculate the best angle/tilt positions of the solar panels, one has to consider the environmental conditions of the area. Many places have big trees and buildings that can shade the solar panels.

For better efficiency of the solar panels, we have to get to areas where maximum sunrays and angle positions can be achieved.

Angle/Tilt Calculation

Solar Panel Angle Calculation

Season	Angle/ Tilt Calculation
Winter	Latitude x 0.9 + 29 degrees
Summer	Latitude x 0.9 - 23.5 degrees
Spring and Fall	Latitude - 2.5 degrees

This figure will help you get the correct angle for solar panels in order to generate the most energy from your solar-powered system.

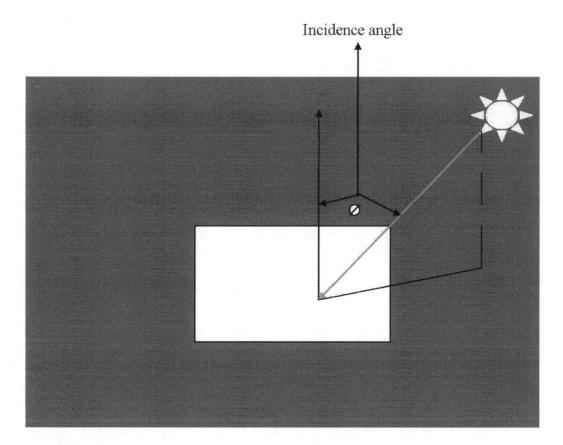

A SKETCH OF SUN'S INCIDENCE ANGLE

Incidence angle

Fig.36

The Sun's Incidence Angle

THE ANGLES IN DEGREES

Study the table of angles below (Sine, Cosine and Tangent)

	0°	30°	45°	60°	90°
sin θ	0	$\frac{1}{2}$	$\frac{\sqrt{2}}{2}$	$\frac{\sqrt{3}}{2}$	1
cos θ	1	$\frac{\sqrt{3}}{2}$	$\frac{\sqrt{2}}{2}$	$\frac{1}{2}$	0
tan θ	0	$\frac{\sqrt{3}}{3}$	1	$\sqrt{3}$	$\pm\infty$

From trigonometry mathematical table

Fig.37

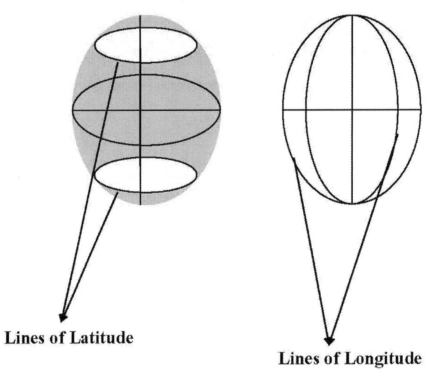

Lines of Latitude

Lines of Longitude

Fig.38(i)

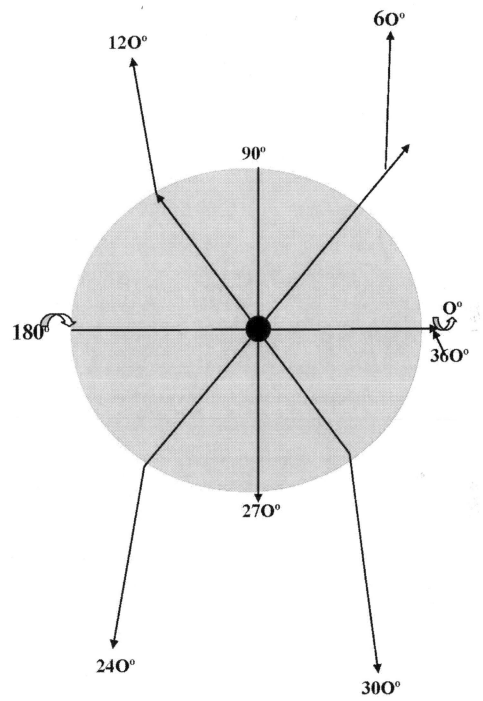

Fig.39(ii)

2π radians equals 360 degrees.

This means that 1 radian = 180/π degrees, and 1 degree = π/180 radians.

Degree in Minutes

One degree = sixty minutes
Sixty seconds = one minute
One degree = sixty arc minutes
Sixty seconds = one minute
Sixty seconds = one′
Fifteen seconds = ? 15/60 = 0.25 minutes
Example: 47°, 33′, 15 seconds

= 33+ 0.25 = 33.25′
1 degree = 60 arc minutes
? = 33.25′ = 0.554°
Thus 47° + 0.554° = 47.554°

The figure is the relationship between degrees and radians for the most common angles in the unit circle measured in the anticlockwise direction from the point to the right of the vertex. The ordered pair is degree measure and radian measure.

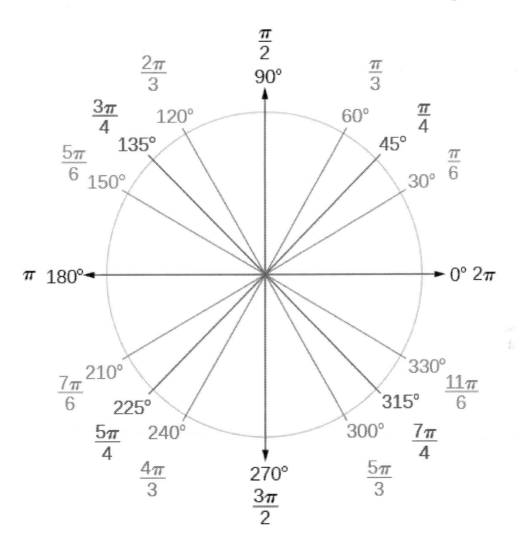

The figure above is from cnx.org

The 2Π radians equals 360 degrees. This means that 1 radian = 180/Π degrees and 1 degree = Π/180 radians.

Compass

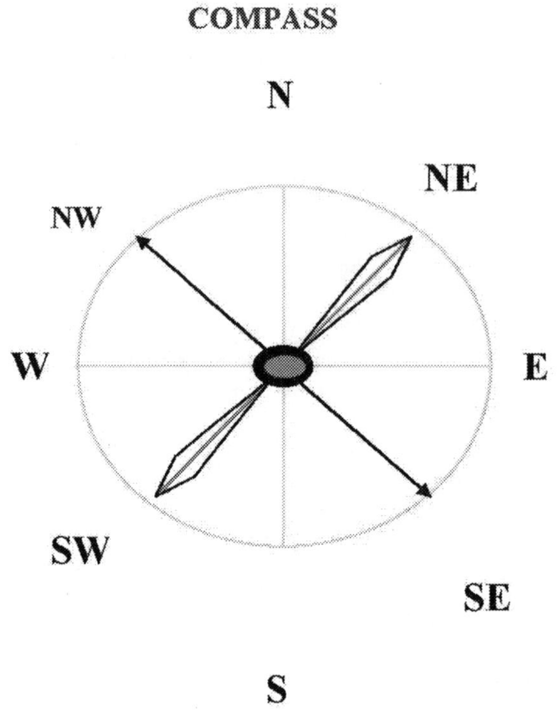

COMPASS

N

NE

NW

W   E

SW

SE

Fig.40

S

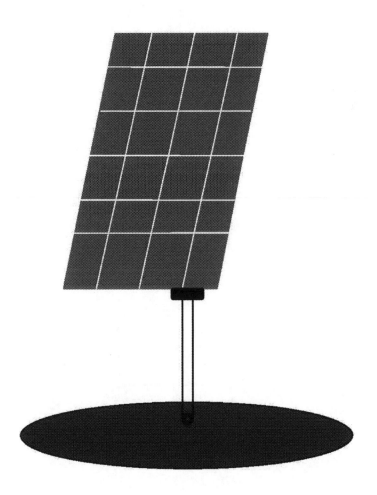

Fig.41   Mounted Solar Panel

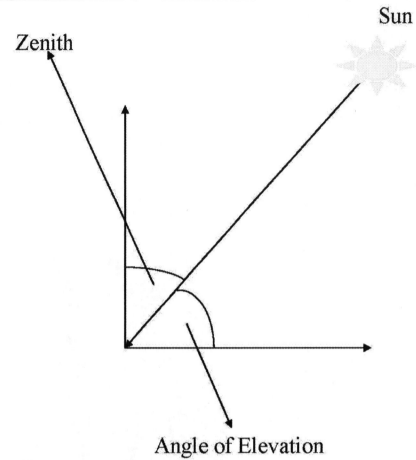

Fig.42

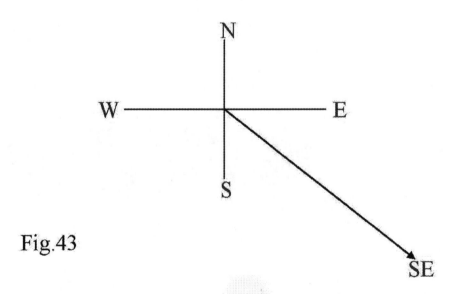

Fig.43

Directing Solar Modules during Installation

Solar modules will get their best striking sunrays when in the direction of the South Pole, at a good angle of inclination.

From the diagram, one can notice that the sun rises in the east and sets in the west.

The sun, the moon, the planets, and the stars all rise in the east and set in the west.

This is because the earth spins towards the east.

Diffuse and Direct Solar Radiations

The sketch below explains diffuse and direct solar radiations

DIFFUSE AND DIRECT SOLAR RADIATION

The sketch below explains Diffuse and Direct solar radiations

Diffuse reflection

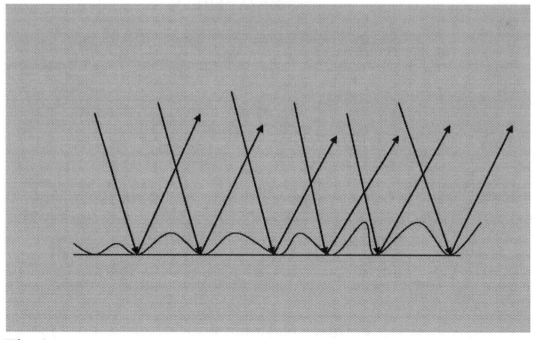

Fig.44

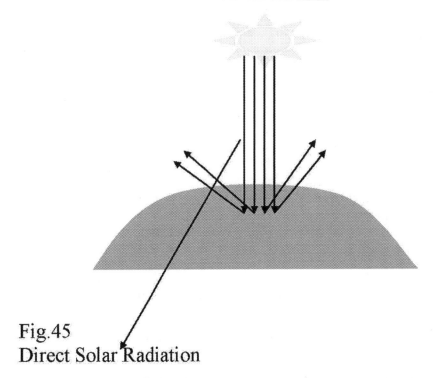

Fig.45
Direct Solar Radiation

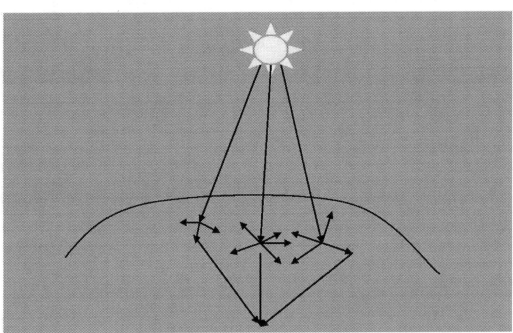

Scattered solar sun radiation

Diffuse solar radiation

Fig.46

Direct solar radiation comes directly from the sun and is measured by a pyrheliometer installed on a solar tracker.

Diffuse solar radiation is scattered by clouds, dust, and molecules.

Global solar radiation is the summation of this scattered radiation falling on a horizontal surface, and it is measured by a pyranometer.

Angler Variations

The angle θ between the zenith and the direct solar beam shows the maximum radiation on the earth's surface.

The air mass = $1/\cos\theta$

AM 0 is the value of its solar radiation outside the earth's atmosphere (1.350 KWm-2).

AM 1 is the value on the earth's surface when the sun is overhead (1KWm-2).

Europe has an air mass of AM 1.5.

Determine the air mass number when the sun is at an altitude of thirty-three degrees.

Remember that air mass = $1/\cos\theta$.

CHAPTER 15

Different Types of Solar Modules (Panels)

We have different kinds of solar panels, which can help you to determine the right solar panel for your installation.

- Monocrystalline silicon solar panels are costly and are the most efficient solar panels. These solar modules are also called single-silicon or mono-silicon panels.

- Polycrystalline solar modules (polycrystalline silicon panels) are less efficient and not as costly as the monocrystalline solar panels. These panels are also called multi-silicon or multi-crystalline panels.

Building Integrated Photovoltaics (BIPV) are the most expensive and are designed to be part of the building. They look like building-roof tiles. Although costly, they are much less efficient and do not last long.

- Thin film modules use thin layers of photovoltaic material like amorphous silicon. They are much cheaper than the other kinds of solar panels but are also less efficient.

- Solar hot water solar panel collectors make use of heat from the sun. They can be used to heat water but do not produce electricity.

Different Forms of Mounting Solar Modules

DIFFERENT FORMS OF MOUNTING SOLAR MODULES

Fig.47

Blue Sun Solar

Fig.48

Fig.49

Roof Mounting of Solar Modules

(a)

Fig.50   Blue Sun Solar

(b)

Blue Sun Solar

Fig.51

(c)

Blue Sun Solar

Fig.52

(d)

Blue Sun Solar Structural installation formation

Fig.53

PV Roof Mounting Systems

Solar Panels: Paralle/Series Connections Sketch

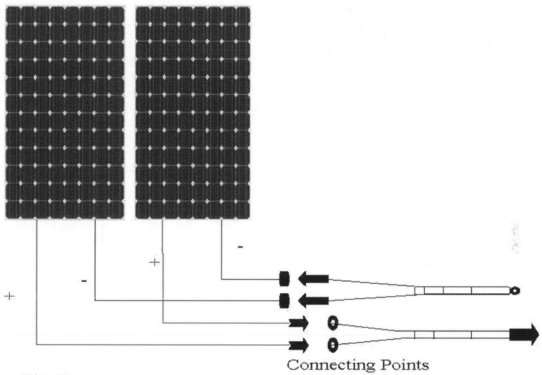

Connecting Points

Fig.54

CHAPTER 16

Solar Panels: Parallel/ Series Connections

Note: For parallel connections, the system is + to +, - to -, meaning to connect all the positive signs to positive and all the negative signs to negative poles. Furthermore, when you want to make your connections in parallel, that means the voltage remains the same while the current (I) in amperes increases. For example, output voltage equals eighteen volts each of two solar panels, and output current (I) of each of the solar panels equals 15A.

If we shunt each of the solar panels in parallel, the total voltage will still be eighteen. In this case the current will be I (1) + I (2) = 15A + 15A =30A.

Fig. 1: V =18v, I=15A
Fig. 2: V=18v, I =15A

Parallel Connections

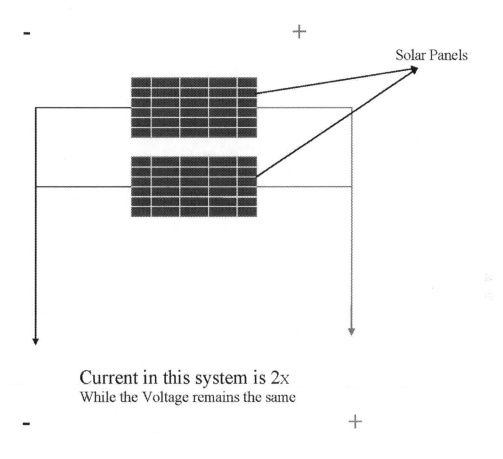

Solar Panels

Current in this system is 2x
While the Voltage remains the same

Fig.55

In this system, one finds out that the current has increased two times, while the voltage remains the same.

Solar Array Connection in Parallel with Connectors

Solar Array Connections and Parallel Connectors

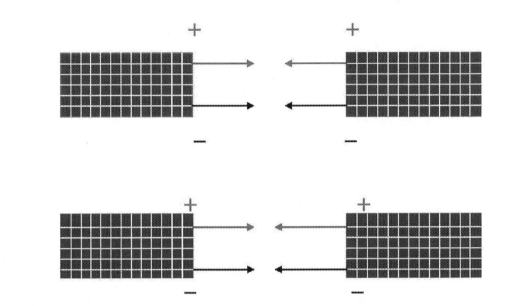

Fig.56

Here one finds out that all the positive poles are connected together with the help of solar connectors and all the negative poles are connected together with the help of solar connectors too.

+ to + and − to − system connections (plus to plus and minus to minus) connections.

This implies positive pole to positive pole and negative pole to negative pole.

All the positive poles are connected together with the help of solar positive connectors, and all the negative poles are connected together with the help of solar negative connectors.

+ to + and - to - system connection

Plus pole to plus pole and minus pole to minus pole

Solar-Panel Series Connections

One has to bear in mind that when connecting solar panels in series, one wants to increase the voltage, while the current remains the same.

This always implies the (-) pole to the (+) pole.

Thus the voltage increases while the current remains the same.

Below are some examples of the series connections:

Solar Panel Series Connections

One has to bear in mind that connecting solar panels in series, one wants to increase the voltage while the current remains the same

This implies that the **(-)** pole to will be connected to the **(+)** pole always

Thus, the voltage increases while the current remains the same.

Below are some sketches of Series connections.

PV ARRAY

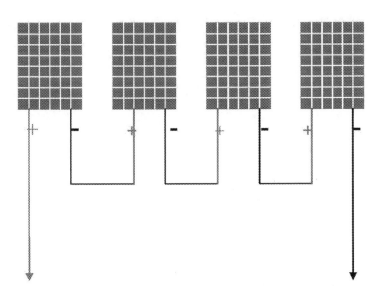

Fig.57

Connection of Batteries in Series

Negative wire

Positive wire

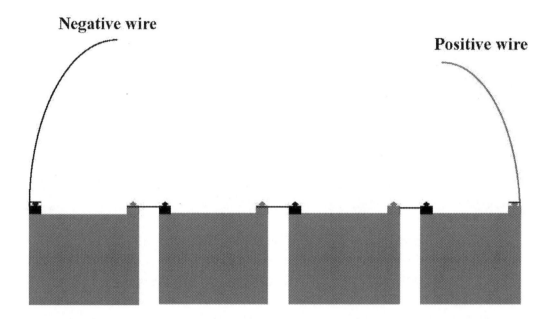

Fig.58

In figure 58, the batteries are connected in series.

CHAPTER 17

Identical Solar Cells

Identical solar cells have to be connected for good performance. It is important to select the poles well, the (+) and (-) poles.

The solar panels should be inclined at the same angle and avoid shading the solar panels. Furthermore, select the cables according to the distance of the solar panels and know the cross-sectional area of the cables.

Connecting different solar panels is done by considering the output voltage of the solar panels. However, if they have the same voltage but a different current, you can connect them. In other words, if they have different voltage values, it is not advisable. Please do not shunt them.

When you have many solar panels to be connected, you have to consider the current value. If your current value is more than 80A, you have to compromise your system by combining parallel and series connections and thus increase both voltage and current simultaneously. Then increase your voltage to twenty-four and forty-eight.

Below are some examples.

Identical Solar Cells

Fig.59

Solar Panel Series / Parallel Connection

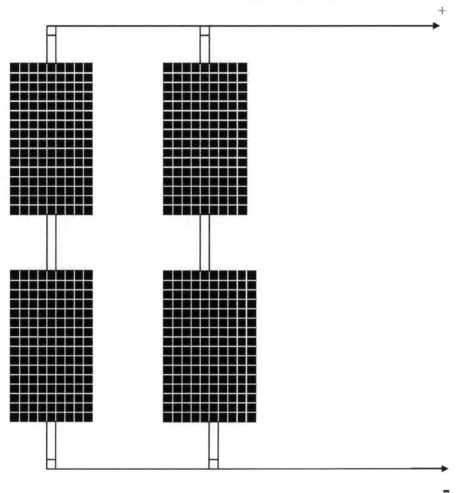

V total = 2V
I total = 2I

Parallel combination of batteries

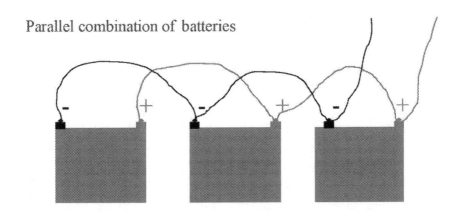

Parallel/Series Combination

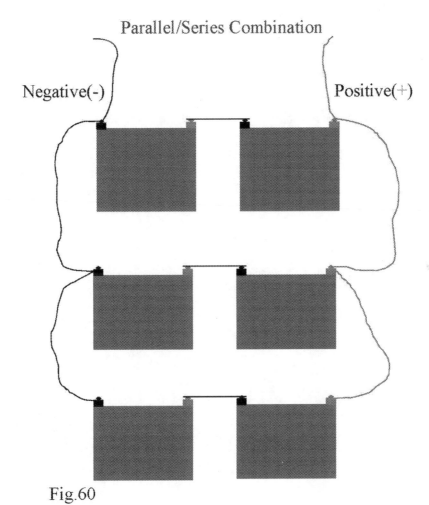

Negative(-)

Positive(+)

Fig.60

CHAPTER 18

Battery Banks

Battery banks allow you to store the energy generated with solar or wind set-up systems. A solar set-up system or array will generate power in the daytime when the sun shines but will stop generating power when the sun goes down at night. Thus the power generated in the daytime will be saved in the battery bank and can then be used at night.

Furthermore, the batteries in a renewable energy should be deep-cycle batteries, which can last a long time.

Deep-cycle batteries are specially made to release energy and to recharge on a regular basis. They withstand a series of circular use before wearing out completely.

Batteries sometimes discharge and get too low, but the use of charge controllers, which check the flow when the battery gets to a level of 50 per cent, are an advantage. Note that car batteries are not advisable for renewable energy systems.

Examples of battery banks:

Example of Battery Bank

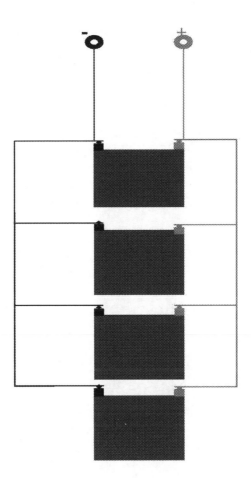

Fig.61

Fig. 61 Here, the current increased while the voltage remained constant (parallel connection)

The Work of Battery Banks

Battery banks are connected to charge controllers, which act like a middle tap, diverting power if the battery reaches its capacity. The charge controller stands between the solar panels or wind turbines and the battery.

The energy generated by the wind turbine or solar array comes as DC and is stored in the battery. The battery output is connected to the inverter.

The DC is now converted to AC by the inverter so that it can be used in homes or the grid system.

Load, Time, Voltage, and Ampere Hour Calculations

Note that if you are given the load (watts), maybe from LED lights, the voltage of the battery, and the ampere hour, you can definitely calculate the time the light system will last per day.

Load x time/battery volt (system voltage)
= ampere hour (AH)
For example, when your solar array system has LED lights of three by thirty watts, twelve volts battery of 180-ampere hour, how long will the light glow?

It will be 90(W) x T / 12V = 180 AH

T is time.
T = 12 V x 180 AH / 90 W
T = 24 hours

Remember, watt = power = IV
V = voltage
A = amper = *I* (current)

CHAPTER 19

Solar Connectors

There are different types of solar connectors that can be used to connect solar panel arrays.

SOLAR CONNECTORS

There are different types of solar connectors that can be used to connect solar panel arrays.

Fig.62

Fig.63   Solar Connector connected to solar panels

Solar Connector connected to solar panels

Solar Connectors

Fig.64

Solar Panel Connectors

Fig.65

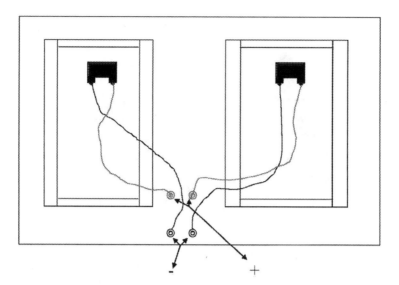

The solar panel negative and positive connecting points

Fig.66

Solar connectors and solar panels showing the + and – poles

Other sketches of solar panel connectors are shown below:

MC4: Male and Female connectors

Parallel Connection

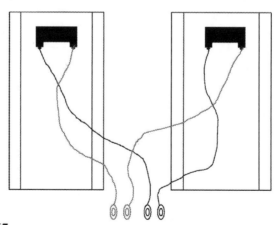

Fig.67

Plus (+) to plus (+) Connection

Minus (-) to Minus (-) Connection

Series Connection

Series Connections

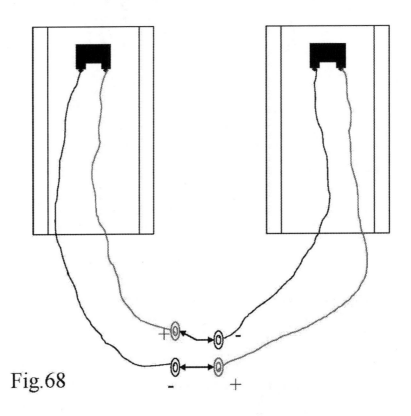

Fig.68

CHAPTER 20

Power Inverters

Power inverters provide power to run household electric devices. These inverters are available in different voltages and loads. The inverter converts the direct current DC to AC (alternating current), which then can be used in household appliances. The inverter also has a function of checking excessive power, voltage, or current by cutting the contact or tripping off.

Efficiency of the Power Inverter

The quality of the output waveform (230VAC) from the inverter determines its efficiency.

Types of power inverters: There are three kinds of inverters based on the output waveforms:

- The sine wave

- Modified sine wave

- Square wave inverters

The sine wave: This is the AC waveform which comes from the domestic lines and from the generator.

The main advantage of the sine wave inverter is that all household appliances are designed to operate in sine wave AC.

The advantages of the sine wave inverters are that they can form soft temporal rise voltage and that they lack harmonic oscillations which can cause unwanted counter forces on engines, interference on radio, and surge current on condensers too.

The modified sine wave inverter is developed to simulate sine wave inverters. This is so because the sine wave is very expensive. This waveform consists of a positive voltage, dropping to zero for a short period of time and then dropping again to negative voltage. It then goes back to zero again and returns to positive.

This short stop at zero volts gives more power to 50 Hz fundamental frequency of AC than the simple square wave. This type of inverter can power most household appliances adequately. It is more economical but poses problem for most appliances like microwave ovens, laser printers, most musical instruments, and digital clocks.

Square Wave Power Inverters

The square wave power inverter is the simplest form of output wave available. Furthermore, it is the cheapest of the other ones too. This type of inverter can run simple appliances without problems.

Terms Related to Inverters

Watt is the value of how much power is used by a device. This is the voltage times the amps (i.e., $P = VI$ or $P = IV$, where p is power, v is voltage, and I is current).

Note that if the device takes fifteen amps at a voltage of 12 V DC, the power is 180 watts.

A watt-hour or kilowatt-hour (kWh) is the number of watt times or how many hours the device is used. Thus if the device uses twenty watts for five hours, then it is 100 Wh = 0.1KWh.

Ampere measures the electrical current. This is very important in order to determine the size of the wire to be used or to connect to the inverter or battery. Note that low-gauge wires will just heat up and burn or melt if heavy current flows through them to the battery.

Ampere hour (AH)

This is ampere times time, and the measure of the battery capacity which determines the backup time of the inverter. Inverters are denoted by VA. For example: 300 VA, 500 VA, 1000 VA, 1500 VA, and so on.

Inverters need peak or surge power. Peak power is the maximum power that the inverter can supply, usually for a short period.

Selection of the Inverter Size

The inverter size can be determined by the following formula: VA = watt x inverter loss. Inverter loss is 1.15. Thus if the total load connected to the inverter is 200 watts, the minimum inverter size will be 200 wx 1.15 = 230VA; therefore, a 300 VA is suitable for the load.

Some Inverter Pictures

Pure Sine Wave Form

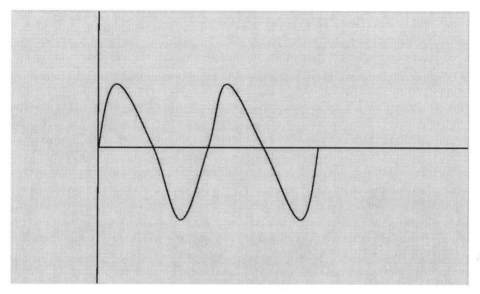

Fig.69

Inverter Sketch

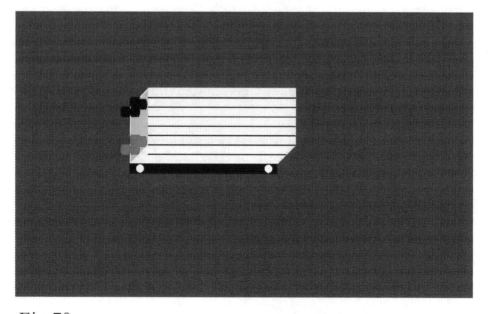

Fig.70

Inverter picture, inverters are denoted in
watt, eg, 500w, 1000w, 2500w etc.

Solar Panel, Battery, Inverter, and Household Electric Bulbs

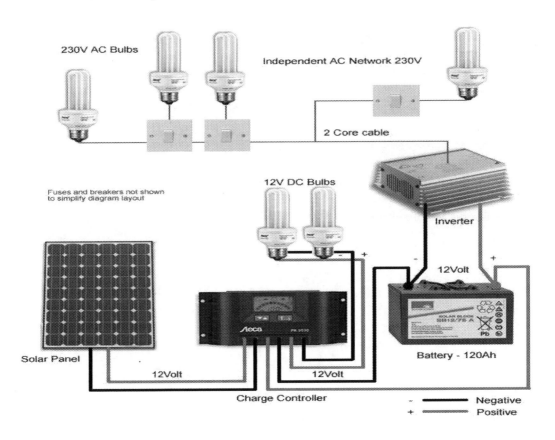

Fig.71 www.kitenergie.com

Energy light bulbs

Fig.72

CHAPTER 21

Current and Voltage Measuring Instruments

Ammeter: Ammeter is an instrument used in measuring electric current. Current (I) is measured in amperes (A).

Some sketches of ammeter:

A sketch of ammeter

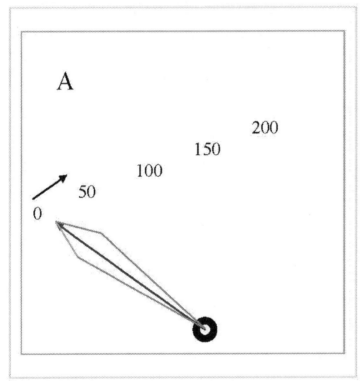

Fig.73

This is a typical example of multimeter. This multimeter instrument can be used to measure voltage, current, and resistance.

A multimeter, or a multitester, called a volt ohmmeter, is an electrical instrument which combines several measuring functions in one unit. An example of multimeter instrument which measures voltage, current, and resistance. These functions are in one VOM (volt ohmmeter).

Voltage Measuring Instrument

Voltage across variable or different points

- This means that when you measure voltage, you measure the difference between two points in space.

Voltmeter Representation

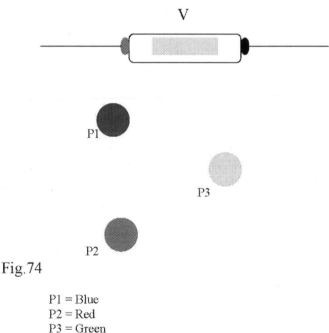

Voltage Measuring Instrument

Voltage across variables or different points
Thus, measuring voltage signifies measuring the difference between two specific points in space.

Representation of Voltmeter

V

P1

P3

P2

Fig.74

P1 = Blue
P2 = Red
P3 = Green

Example

P1 (blue)

P2 (red)

P3 (green)

Let us look at these three points. They can be anything and just located in a circuit. One has to note that there is a voltage difference between any two of these points which can be measured. We have many choices of voltage differences, such as blue/red, red/green, green/blue or red, green, green/blue, blue/red.

For our introduction to the voltmeter, we need to be aware of three items on the voltmeter.

Here is what you have to put consider when using the voltmeter:

- The result of the measurement is displayed.

- The meter can be either analogue or digital.

- When analogue, you need to read a reading off a scale. When digital, it will usually have an LED or LCD display panel where you can see what the voltage measurement reads.

- Note that the positive input terminal is typically red.

- Note that the negative input terminal is usually black.

Circuits

Take an example from three points. These points may be anything and may be located in a circuit. Wherever they are, there is a voltage difference between any two of these points, and you could theoretically measure the voltage difference between any two of these points. There are three different choices for voltage differences.

We have the same three points, but now they are points within a circuit. In this circuit, the battery will produce a current that flows through the two resistors in a series.

CIRCUITS

Considering three points located in a circuit, there is a voltage difference between any two of these points and it can be measured

Mostly, there are three different choices of voltage differences.

In a circuit as illustrated below, using a battery, the battery will produce a current that flows through the two resistors in series.

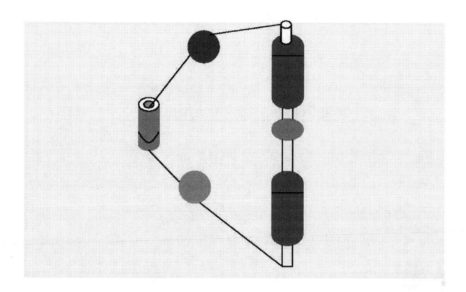

Fig.75

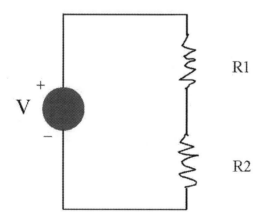

Fig.76

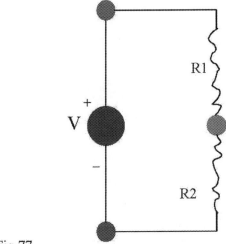

Fig.77

Measurement of voltage

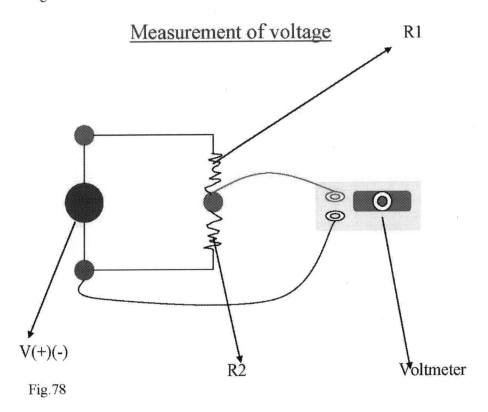

Fig.78

The same circuit with the measurement points:

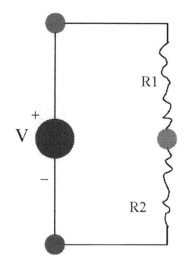

Fig.77

Measurement of voltage

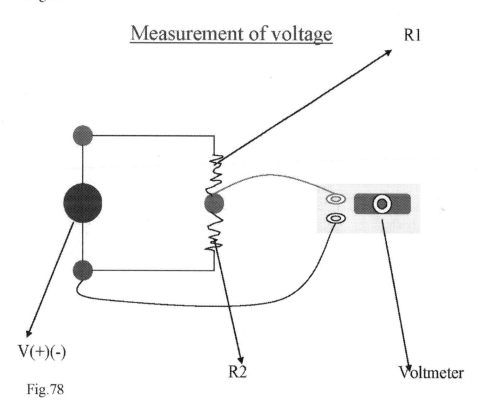

Fig.78

When you want to measure the voltage across R₂, figure 77 is the connection.

Physically, the circuit will look like the diagram in figure 78.

CHAPTER 22

Quadrants (First, Second, Third, and Fourth Quadrants)

Indication of Quadrants

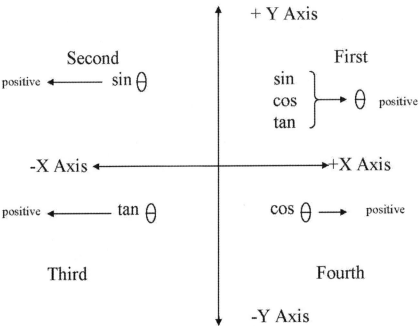

Fig.79

When you observe the quadrants in the sketch above, one finds out that in the first quadrant, sine, cosine and tangent are all positive. In the second quadrant, sine is positive while cosine and tangent are negative.

In the third quadrant, sine and cosine are negative while tangent is positive.

In the fourth quadrant, cosine is positive while sine and tangent are negative.

SOHCAHTOA

Sin = opp/hyp
Cos = adj/hyp
Tan = opp/adj

Sohcahtoa
Sine = OPP/HYP Tan = OPP/ ADJ
Cosine =ADJ/HYP

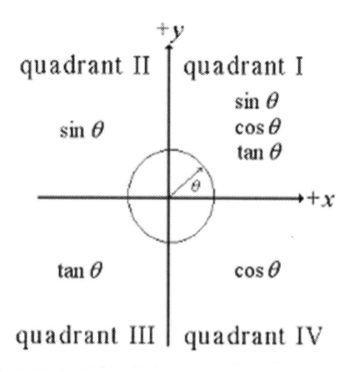

In the first quadrants, sine, cosine, and tangents are all positive. In the second quadrant, sine is positive, while cosine and tan are negative. In the third quadrant, sine is negative; cosine is also negative, while tan is positive. In the fourth quadrant, cosine is positive, while sine and tangents are negative.

CHAPTER 23

Longitude/Latitude

Longitude and Latitude Lines

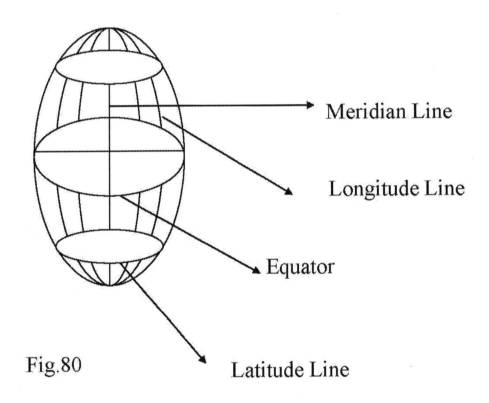

Meridian Line

Longitude Line

Equator

Fig.80   Latitude Line

Location of Areas

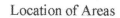

Location of Areas

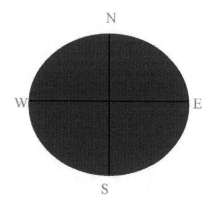

Fig.81

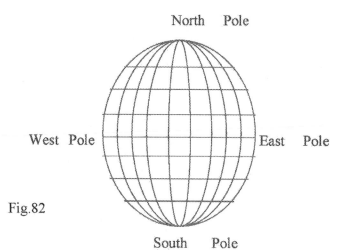

Fig.82

In the above diagram, one can easily locate the lines of longitudes and latitudes.

The diagrams above show the lines of longitude, latitude, and the equator.

Location of Continents on the Hemisphere

Location of Continents on the Hemisphere

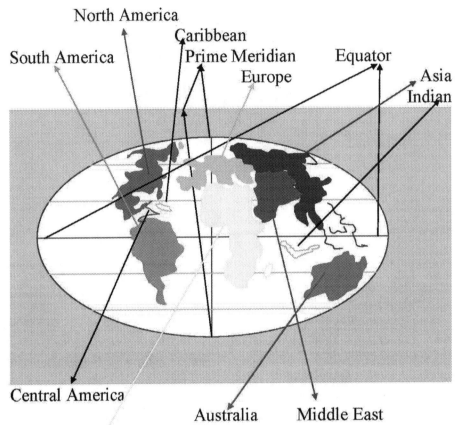

Fig.83

Location of Africa in the Hemisphere for example, one can observe from the sketches above that both the equator and prime meridian run through Africa.

Location of Africa on the Hemisphere, one can observe from the sketches above, that both equator and Prime Meridian run through Africa.

Calculations of Longitudes and Latitudes

Remember this when you want to find the difference in longitudes. Whether a longitude of 118 degrees and a longitude of 117 degrees, forty-five minutes, you need to subtract the longitudes; the equator has zero degrees. From this, you have a fifteen-minute difference in the longitudes.

If you also want to calculate the difference in the latitudes, maybe a latitude of thirty degrees and a latitude of twenty-five, the difference is five degrees.

Thus longitude and longitude then subtract. Furthermore, longitude latitude or latitude longitude then add.

For this, NS (add) SN (add), ES (add) SE (add), EW (add), SW (add) WS (add)

NN, SS, EE, WW, subtraction is always the case.

Calculations of Longitude and Latitudes

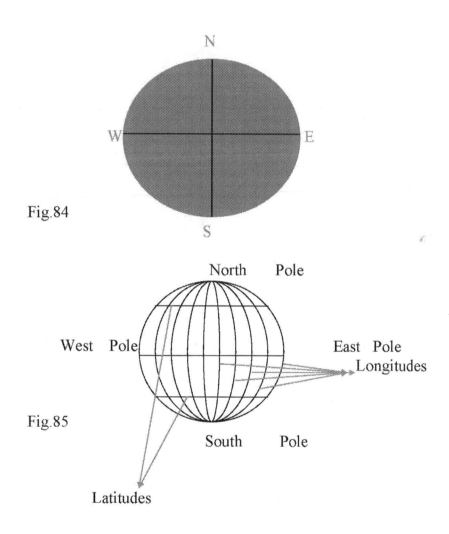

Fig.84

Fig.85

CHAPTER 24

Horsepower

Air conditioning power is rated by its horsepower. Before installing a cooling system, one has to make sure that the horsepower is converted to the required power unit in order to enable one to know the actual load to be used.

1000W = 1 KW

1 Horsepower = 746 Watts

When 1 horsepower is equivalent to 746watts, then this is the equivalent of 1 watt:

1 hp = 746w

1w = ?

1w x 1hp / 746w = 0.0013405 HP

Example: If you have an air conditioning system of 2.5 horsepower, this will be its equivalent in watts:

1hp = 746 w

2.5hp = ?

Therefore, the equivalent in watts will be 1865 W.

CHAPTER 25

Energy Units

SI multiples for watt-hour (W. h)

SI multiples for watt hour (W·h)					
Submultiples			**Multiples**		
Value	**Symbol**	**Name**	**Value**	**Symbol**	**Name**
10^{-3}	mW·h	milliwatt hour	10^3	kW·h	kilowatt hour
10^{-6}	μW·h	microwatt hour	10^6	MW·h	megawatt hour
			10^9	GW·h	gigawatt hour
			10^{12}	TW·h	terawatt hour
			10^{15}	PW·h	petawatt hour

(Wikipedia)

The kilowatt-hour (symbolized kWh) is a unit of energy equivalent to one kilowatt (1 kW) of power expended for one hour.

$$\text{kW} \cdot \text{h} = (3600\,\text{s})[\text{kW}] = 3600\,[\text{s}]\left[\frac{\text{kJ}}{\text{s}}\right] = 3600\,\text{kJ} = 3.6\,\text{MJ}$$

(Wikipedia)
1 kilojoule = $10^{3\,\text{joules}}$
1 megajoule = $10^{6\,\text{joules}}$
3600 KJ = 3600 J X $10^{3\,\text{joules}}$
1 megajoule = $10^{6\,\text{joules}}$
? = 3600J X $10^{3\,\text{joules}}$
3600J X $10^{3\,\text{J}}$ X 1MJ
$10^{6\,\text{J}}$
= 3.6 MJ

CHAPTER 26

Always Obey Safety Signs (AOSS)

The most safety hazards one has to bear in mind are

1. Physical hazards, such as explosives, flammable liquids, oxidizing liquids, corrosive materials, and compressed gases, electric shock. Etc.

2. Health hazards such as skin corrosion, toxicity, irritation, aspiration hazard, etc.

free clipart

Fig.86   Fire hazard sign

Fire Hazards

CHAPTER 27

Maintenance

- Preventive maintenance is recommended every year.

- Always refer to manuals and have consultations when you are not sure about something concerning the system.

- Visual inspections and electrical connections of the PV Modules should always be observed.

- Check the uniformity of the current and voltage of the modules.

- Check basement or support structures, making sure the mechanical stability, weathering, moving parts, and corrosion are also checked.

- Make sure the modules are not full of dust in order to avoid reduction in efficiency.

- Make sure there is room for free flow of air in the solar array system.

- Always check the impact of rodents in the solar array area.

- Check cabinet and insulation (heating/melting)—switchgear.

- Try to check the batteries, acid level, electrolytic density, and corrosion.

- For the inverters, always follow the manufacturer's instructions.

- Make sure the nuts and bolts are tightly fixed and replace any that you feel are not good.

- Make sure that the structures that will hold the solar modules are strongly built to avoid falling or bending, thereby causing hazards; the tilt angles of the solar array may change due to the bending too.

- Application of paints or adhesives should be avoided.

- Keep children away from installations at all times.

- Avoid wearing metallic rings, watches, and so forth, during solar photovoltaic system installations.

- Adhere to the use of insulated tools and insulating globes.

- Use the same type of modules during installation.

- Do not stand on solar modules.

- Remember that short circuit currents and open circuit voltages should always be multiplied by a factor of 1.25 when determining the component voltage ratings, conductor capacity, fuse sizes, and size of controls connected to the module system.

- Reference National Electrical Code (NEC), with additional multiplying factor of 125 per cent (80 per cent derating).

- Avoid shadowing of the modules at all times. Each cell in a module must pass the same current.

- Remember that a shaded cell will generate less current and then will act as a load for the photo current in the string. In this case, the shaded cell will heat up and will reduce the voltage output.

- Avoid this heat up and voltage output reduction by adding a bypass diode across the strings or across the module to create a current path. This introduces a small voltage drop but avoids local heating of the shaded cell and limits the array's output reduction. Sometimes a diode may fail as a circuit.

CHAPTER 28

Safety Precautions

The installer of solar systems or wind turbines should observe or conform to all safety rules before installing.

- Observe electrical and mechanical requirements before installation of solar or turbine systems.

- Try to avoid shock at all times.

- When wiring modules are exposed to sunlight, you have to be very careful, mostly when disconnecting wires connected to modules exposed to sunlight.

- Make sure that the solar array system is earthed to protect the solar system from thunder and lightning.

Example of thunder and lightning schematic diagram below:

clipart.me

CHAPTER 29

Wind Energy (Wind Power)

Wind power is generated from airflow, using turbines to produce electrical energy.

Also an alternative to fossil fuels, it is quite renewable in nature and does not pollute the environment during operations.

When there are huge convection currents in the earth's atmosphere due to heat energy from the sun, then there is wind. This means that as long as the sun shines, there will be wind. On the earth's surface is land and water. However, when the sun shines, the air over the land heats up more quickly than the air over the water does. The heated air, which has low density (is lighter), rises, and the cooler air, which has high density, falls and replaces the air over the land.

In the night, the reverse is the case. The air over the water is warm and has less density, so it rises and is replaced by cooler air of higher density from the land.

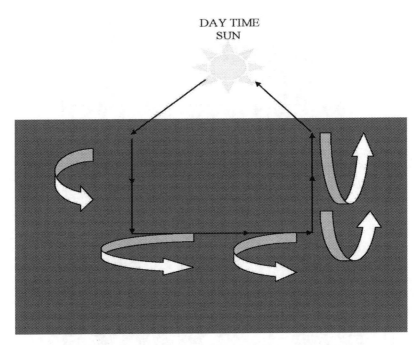

**Fig.87 Warm air over the land rises and is being replaced by cooler air
This is due to the convection currents**

Warm air over the land rises and is replaced by cooler air. This is due to the convection currents.

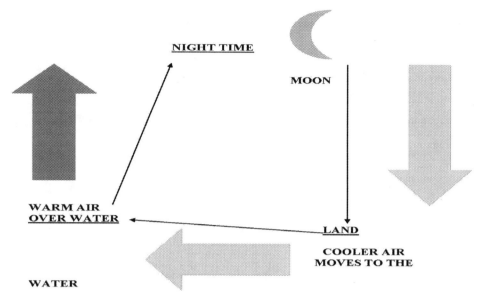

Fig.88

The movement of the air is known as wind. This wind has high kinetic energy which can be transferred into electrical energy using wind turbines. The blades of the wind turbines rotate through a spin shaft. This spin shaft is connected to a generator which generates electricity.

OFFSHORE WIND POWER

This refers to the installation of wind turbines in large bodies of water to produce or generate electricity. Here, frequent powerful winds are made use of in the area and has low aesthetic impact on the landscape based wind turbine projects.

The movement of the air is known as wind. This wind has high kinetic energy which can be transferred into electrical energy using wind turbines. The blades of the wind turbines rotate through a spin shaft. This spin shaft is connected to a generator which generates electricity.

Offshore Wind Power

This refers to the installation of wind turbines in large bodies of water to produce or generate electricity. Frequent powerful winds are made use of in the area, and they have low aesthetic impact on the landscape-based wind turbine projects.

The Floating Wind Turbine

This is an offshore wind turbine installed on a floating structure, which allows the turbine to generate electricity in water depths in the way that there are no depth bottom installed anchors or towers. A typical example is from the figure below.

The floating wind turbine

This kind is an offshore wind turbine installed on a floating structure which allows the turbine to generate electricity in water depths in a way that there are no depth bottom installed anchors or towers.

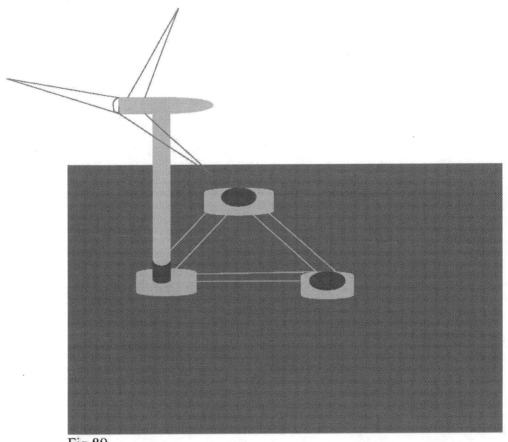

Fig.89
The simple sketch above shows how the floating wind turbine will look like in water.

Floating wind turbine

The world's second full-scale floating wind turbine (and first to be installed without the use of heavy-lift vessels), WindFloat, operating at rated capacity (2 MW) approximately five kilometres offshore of Aguçadoura, Portugal.

(Wikipedia)

Wind Power Structures

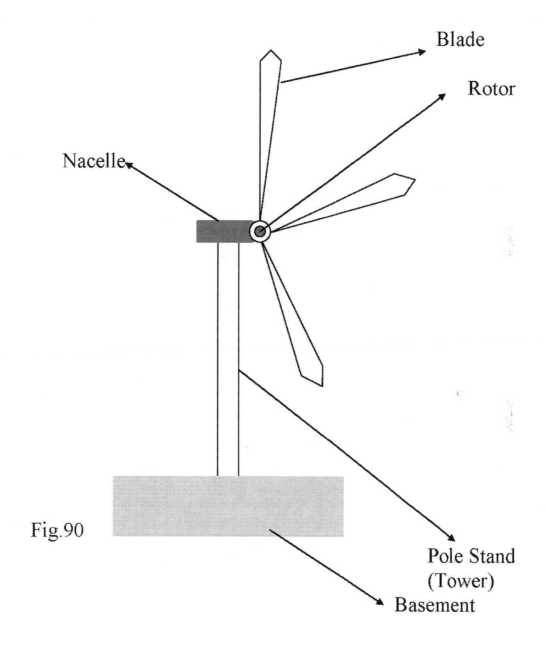

Wind Power Structure

Blade

Rotor

Nacelle

Fig.90

Pole Stand
(Tower)

Basement

The graph of power of wind and its speed

Wind power curves

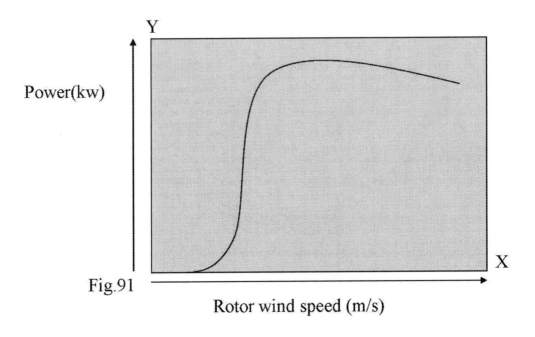

Power(kw)

Fig.91

Rotor wind speed (m/s)

Turbine Blade Lengths

The swept area of blade

Diameter of Rotor

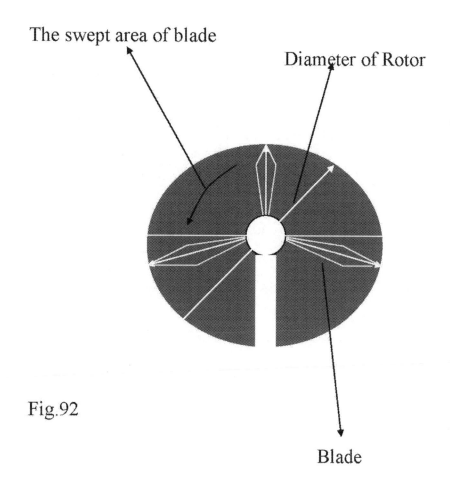

Fig.92

Blade

Wind Speed

When considering wind speed, the speed at which the rotor and the blade assembly begin their rotational movement, we also have the cut-in speed. This is the minimum wind speed at which the wind turbine will generate usable power. For most turbines, the wind speed is between seven and ten miles per hour.

Rated speed is the minimum speed at which the wind turbine will generate its required or designated rated power. The rated speed for most machines is in the range of twenty-five to thirty-five miles per hour. Furthermore, the power output from wind turbines increases as the wind increases between cut-in and rated wind speeds.

The wind turbine output varies with the wind speed. This can be shown through power curves or graphs, as illustrated in the wind power curves.

When there is a very high wind speed—for example, between forty-five and eighty miles per hour—most wind turbines stop power generation and shut down. The wind speed at which the shutdown occurs is called cut-out speed or furling speed.

This is a safety remedy that checks the damage of the turbine machine.

Furthermore, in some turbine machines, a wind sensor activates an automatic brake.

Note also that when the wind speed is doubled, you get more energy. This is one of the reasons for a taller wind tower, thereby increasing the energy derivation. The power outut is usually denoted in watts.

Rotational Kinetic Power of Wind Turbines and Wind Speed

E = kinetic energy (j)
M = mass (kg)
P = density ρ (kg/m³)
A = swept area (m²)
V = wind speed (m/s)
Cp = power coefficient
P = power (watts)
R = radians (m)

Therefore, dm/dt = flow rate of the mass (kg/s)
X = distance (metre)
dE/dt = rate of energy flow, which is in joules (J/S)
t = time in seconds(s)

Following this, under a constant acceleration of an object, the kinetic energy of an object with mass (m) and velocity (v) is equal to the work done in the displacement of the object from its initial rest position to a distance (s) which was acted upon by a force (F).

E = W = FS = force x distance
From Newton's law
F = ma
Thus E = mas, equation (1) from equations of motion:

4 Equations of Motion

$V = u + at$
$S = ut + 1/2at^2$
$S = 1/2t (v + u)$
$v^2 = u^2 + 2as$

From the fourth equation, $a = (v+u)(v-u)/2s$
However, the initial velocity of the object is zero.
The initial velocity is U, so U=0

Therefore, $a=\dfrac{v^2}{2S}$

Put (a) in equation (1)
$E = \frac{1}{2}mv^2$ equation (2)
Thus the power in wind is the rate of energy change.
Power (P) = $dE/dt = 1/2v^2dm/dt$ ... equation (3)
This is because mass flow rate is given by
$dm/dt = PAdx/dt$
The rate of change of distance is given as $dx/dt=Vel =V$
Therefore, $dm/dt = PAV$
From equation 3, the power can be shown as power (P) = $1/2PAv^3$ Equation (4)

Note that no wind turbine can convert more than 16/27 (59.3 per cent of the kinetic energy of the wind into mechanical energy in turning of a rotor. (This is from Albert Betz and is called Betz's law or limit). In this case, the theoretical maximum power efficiency of any designed wind turbine is 0.59 (not more than 59 per cent of the energy carried by the wind can be extracted by a wind turbine).

This is therefore known as the power coefficient Cpmax = 0.59

The real world limit is just below Betz's limit, and the values are 0.35 to 0.45.

Considering some factors such as bearings, gearbox, generators, and so forth, one will find out that only 10 to 30 per cent of the power of the wind will be converted to usable electricity. Therefore, power extracted from the wind is denoted by power (P extracted) = *0.5PAv³Cp* Equation (5).

Turbine Blade Lengths

Considering the turbine blade lengths, the swept area of the turbine can be derived using the area of a circle, which is as follows:

$$A = \pi \times r^2 \text{ Equation (6)}$$

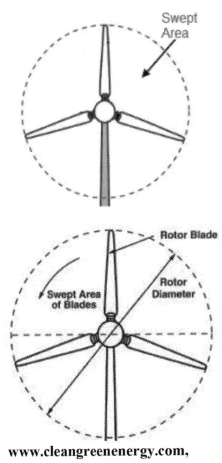

Calculations with a given data given the blade length as 60 m

For instance, at sea level and at 15 °C, the air density is 1.275 kg/m³, the international standard atmosphere (ISA).

Air density at sea level: *ρ=1.275kg/*m

Wind speed = Vel = 12.5 m/s

Power Coefficient Cp assuming = 0.45

Now, if the blade length is equal to the radius

L=r=60m

Thus, A=πr²

3.142X60X60=3.142X3600

=11311.2 m²

The power converted from the wind into Rotational Energy in the turbine will be calculated as follows:

Pextracted =$0.5PAv^3Cp$, which is $0.5x1.275x11311.2x12.5^3x0.45$

6.34 mw (megawatts)

N/B: one megawatt is equivalent to one million watts

REFERENCES

Solar Modules (solar panels)

Bluesun Solar (ref. pictures from David)

SI multiples for watt-hours (w.h), Wikipedia

Turbines

ISA (International Standard Atmosphere)

Betz's law or limit (Albert Betz)

Floating Wind Turbines

SI Units (System International)

Albert Einstein

Mathematical Trigonometry Table

Location of Continents (World Atlas)

Fire Hazards (Free Clipart)

Sketch Drawings (By Engr. Julian K. Igbo)

The Green Organisation

European Energy Centre, Great Britain

Energie Akademie Toggenburg, Switzerland

NEPA (National Electric Power Authority)

NEC (National Electrical Code)

Standard Spectra

IEC (International Electrotechnical Commission)

Azimuth Angle

Geometry of Solar Radiation

APPENDIX

Conversion Units

100cm = 1meter
1 inch = 0.0254meters
1 foot (ft) = 0.3048 metres
1 kilometre (km) = 1000 metres
1 mile = 1609.344 metres
1 acre = 4047m^2 = 43,560ft^2 = 4840yd^2 = 0.4047 hectares
1 sq km = 247.1 acres = 100 hectares
1 sq m = 640 acres = 259 hectares
1 cubic metre (m3) = 1000 litres (l) = 35.315ft3 = 1.308cubic yard (yd3)

Mass

1000g = 1 kilogramme = 2.2046 pounds (lb)

Pressure

1 pa = N/m^2
1 atm = 1.01325X10^5 equal to 101325.01 pascal.
1 bar = 10^5pa=10^5N/m^2
1 atm = 760mmHg=29.91213 in Hg = 34ftH2O

Degrees

1 degree = 60 mins.
60 seconds = 1 min.
1 degree = 60 arc mins.

Units for Energy

Joule = Newton metre (J = Nm = ws)
1 joule = 0.947817x10^{-3} British thermal unit = 0.27778x10^{-6}Kwh
1 joule = 0.23884x10^{-3}kilo calorie (kcal)
1Kwh = 3.6x10^6J = 3412.14 BTU

1 Kcal = 4186.8 J = 3.96832BTU
1BTU = 1055.06 J

Horsepower

1 horsepower = 746Watts
1000W = 1KW
Flow Rate
M^3/s metre cube per second

ft^3/min cubic foot per minute

Density

Density is equal to mass per unit volume = kg/m^3

Temperature

Kelvin (K), Celsius(°C), and Fahrenheit(°F)
1 degree Celsius = 33.8 degrees Fahrenheit
$T(°C) = (T(°F)-32)×5/9$
or
$T(°C) = (T(°F)-32)/1.8$
$T(K) = T(°C)+273.15$
$T(°F) = T(°C)X1.8+32$
$T(k) = T(°F)+459.67)X5/9$

INDEX

ENGR. JULIAN K. IGBO

B. Eng., Federal University of Technology, Owerri, Nigeria

Solarteur, Energie Akademie Toggenburg, Wattwil, Switzerland

European Energy Centre (EEC), Edinburgh, Napier, University Great Britain

Master's certificates in solar photovoltaics, energy efficiency in buildings, and electrics for renewables

Member European Energy Centre (MEEC)

Member Energy Institute Great Britain

Global Volunteering Programme Award, Honorary Volunteer of the European Energy Centre (EEC)

International Green Apple Awards Winner for Environmental Best Practice 2014

International Green Apple Awards Winner for Environmental Best Practice 2015

Green World Ambassador 2015

Printed in the United States
By Bookmasters